MISSISSIPPI

ON-THE-ROAD HISTORIES

MISSISSIPPI

Ben Wynne

Interlink Books

To the faculty and staff of St. Andrew's Episcopal School in Jackson, Mississippi, who were there while I was a student, 1967–1979.

First published in 2008 by

INTERLINK BOOKS
An imprint of
Interlink Publishing Group, Inc.
46 Crosby Street,
Northampton, MA 01060
www.interlinkbooks.com

Library of Congress Cataloging-in-Publication Data

Wynne, Ben, 1961–
Mississippi / by Ben Wynne.
  p. cm. —(On-the-road histories)
Includes index.
ISBN-13: 978-1-56656-666-7 (pbk.)
ISBN-10: 1-56656-666-5
1. Mississippi—History.
2. Mississippi—Description and travel. I. Title. II. Series.
F341.W94 2006
976.2—dc22

                          2006014578

Printed and bound in China

Mississippi countryside road
© Mario Savoia
Agency: Dreamstime.com

Contents

Acknowledgments

This book could not have been completed without the assistance and support of a number of people to whom I am indebted. I spent many pleasant and productive days in Jackson at the Mississippi Department of Archives and History, thanks to the staff there. They are thoroughly professional and I appreciate their help and hospitality. I would also like to thank all of Mississippi's local historical societies and the volunteers who keep them going. Some of the information for this book came from publications and websites produced by these organizations. Brochures produced by the Mississippi Division of Tourism Development and local chambers of commerce around the state were also very helpful. I would like to acknowledge the special contributions of two good friends: Master wordsmith Bill Fisher of Phoenix, Arizona read much of the manuscript and provided valuable input. I also discussed this project many times with Johnny Greer of Oxford, Mississippi, who provided much appreciated insights into the history of the northern part of the state. Over the last decade or so I have traveled the highways and back roads of Mississippi visiting innumerable historic sites, some grand and some obscure. Many of these trips were made with friends who have unknowingly contributed to this book through their camaraderie and conversations with me. Among them are, in alphabetical order, Lynn Ashford, Brant Helvenston, Alice Lachaussee, John Leggett, Julie Leggett, Marty Lester, Richard Nolen, Scott Poole, Charles Sallis, Ted Smith, and Alan Vestal. Last but certainly not least I would like to thank my wife Carly and Patricia Wynne and Noelle Wynne for their unwavering support in all my endeavors.

INTRODUCTION

Mississippi entered the Union in 1817 as the twentieth state, beginning a history that would be sometimes turbulent and sometimes triumphant. In the centuries before Mississippi became part of the United States—centuries, in fact, before the United States existed—the region was populated by Native Americans who built a vibrant culture with their own traditions, customs, and religious practices. Within a few decades during the seventeenth and eighteenth centuries the various native cultures fell prey almost completely to European intrusion. Some cultures did not survive as the world's great powers struggled to subdue the region and expand their global influence. The land that would become Mississippi passed through French, Spanish, and British hands before the United States took control. Following statehood, thousands of settlers flooded the region. Some came voluntarily, looking for opportunity or adventure, while others, who were enslaved, were forced to make the journey. Sectional arguments related to the institution of slavery brought on the Civil War, which devastated the state and the rest of the South. After the war, and the turbulent Reconstruction period, most Mississippians remained poor for generations, with blacks and whites segregated by custom and law. World War II boosted the state's economy, which continued to evolve until industry overtook agriculture as the state's largest employer. The war also gave way to the civil rights movement, which was at times very painful but in the end led to great change. Afterwards, a new Mississippi emerged.

THE LAND

Like most states, the land within Mississippi's political borders is not uniform. Boundary lines drawn at the time of statehood captured the rich Delta soil bordering the Mississippi River, along with the northeastern hill country and the prairies of the central part of the state. They also captured the pine forests in the south, along with the gulf coast. The fertility and contours of the state's soil would affect patterns of settlement and the development of the state's various regions.

Mississippi's most fertile region is the Delta, a large alluvial plain stretching from the Tennessee state line to Vicksburg along the Mississippi River. Unsettled until the 1850s because of its many swamps and tangled forests, the Delta would not attract a significant population until after the Civil War, when men drained the swamps and built strong levies to control flooding. South of the Delta, in the region around Natchez, are the River Lowlands. The soil there is also fertile, and it provided a good environment for the growth of Mississippi's early plantation economy. The Loess Hills is a strip of hills east of the Delta and the River Lowlands that stretches from the Louisiana border to the Tennessee line, and in most places it has always been conducive to agriculture. In the southeast the vast Piney Woods region provides a good environment for forest growth, but its sandy soil did not allow most nineteenth-century farmers to make a decent living. This area was originally populated by poor, but indefatigable, pioneer stock. Still further south the Gulf Coast is also poorly suited for most crops, but it did serve as the gateway for the first European settlement in the state. The Jackson Prairie, sometimes called the Central Prairie, is located immediately north of the Piney Woods, but, in contrast, it contains good farmland and also good pastures for livestock.

Northeastern Mississippi includes several different types of soil and topographic divisions. The largest division is the North Central Hills, stretching from around Meridian to the Tennessee border. During the antebellum period farmers in this area were only marginally successful at producing crops due to the quality of the soil, and after the Civil War the region continued to struggle. Bordering the North Central Hills to the east are the Flatwoods, a strip of land that has fertile soil but is poorly drained. It contains dense forests, and the population there has been traditionally sparse. Conditions are much better along the Pontotoc Ridge, a strip of good farmland and grazing land cut by numerous streams. Historically, by far the best land in northeastern Mississippi from an agricultural perspective was the Tombigbee Prairie, also called the Black Prairie. This region was an extension of the Alabama Black Belt along the Tombigbee River. Because cotton could be grown there, and because that cotton could be transported to markets by boat on the Tombigbee, the area was among the first settled in Mississippi. Finally, the Tennessee Hills are located in the extreme northeastern part of the state. As the name implies, they are an extension of Middle Tennessee's rolling hills. The soil there is not well suited for farming and federal planners actually consider it part of Appalachia. Before the Civil War the region was fairly isolated from the rest of the state, particularly from the state's economy and cotton culture. There were few slaves in the Tennessee Hills, and most whites who lived there had little respect for slave owners. Though they were overruled, many voiced their support for preserving the Union in 1861.

While lines on a map ultimately united these different regions under a single flag, through the centuries the land itself drew varied groups of inhabitants to what would become the state of Mississippi. Those inhabitants would shape Mississippi's history.

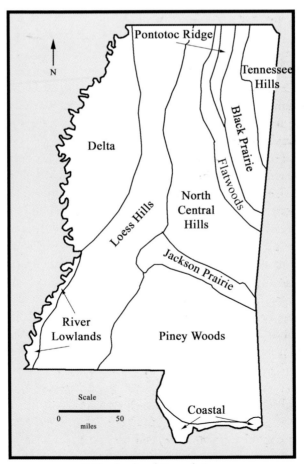

Mississippi Land Area

MISSISSIPPI FACTS

Origin of Name: From several Native American words that translate *Ancient Father of Waters, Beyond Age*, or *Chief River*. The most common translation is *Father of Waters*.

Date of Statehood: December 10, 1817
Nickname: Magnolia State
Capital: Jackson
Population (2000): 2,844,658
Square Miles: 47, 233, including 42 miles of inland water surface.
Avg. Temperature: Monthly average temperatures range from a high of 92.5° to a low of 34.9° (Fahrenheit).

Mississippi Counties

Mississippi Symbols

State motto: Virtute et Armis ("By Valor and Arms")
State bird: Mockingbird
State flower: Magnolia
State tree: Magnolia
State land mammals: White-tailed Deer, Red Fox
State waterfowl: Wood Duck
State fish: Largemouth (Black) Bass
State water mammal: Bottlenose Dolphin
State insect: Honeybee
State butterfly: Spicebush Swallowtail
State wildflower: Coreopis
State stone: Petrified wood
State fossil: Prehistoric whale
State shell: Oyster shell
State dance: Square dance
State song: "Go, Mississippi," words & music by Houston Davis

Mississippi Municipalities
(population 10,000 or more)

Municipality	County	Population
Jackson	Hinds	184,256
Gulfport	Harrison	71,127
Biloxi	Harrison	50,644
Hattiesburg	Forrest	44,779
Greenville	Washington	41,633
Meridian	Lauderdale	39,968
Tupelo	Lee	34,211
Southaven	DeSoto	28,977
Vicksburg	Warren	26,407
Pascagoula	Jackson	26,200
Columbus	Lowndes	25,944
Clinton	Hinds	23,347
Pearl	Rankin	21,961
Starkville	Oktibbeha	21,869
Olive Branch	DeSoto	21,054
Clarksdale	Coahoma	20,645
Ridgeland	Madison	20,173
Natchez	Adams	18,464
Greenwood	Leflore	18,425
Laurel	Jones	18,393
Long Beach	Harrison	17,320
Ocean Springs	Jackson	17,225

Brandon	Rankin	16,436
Moss Point	Jackson	15,851
Grenada	Grenada	14,879
Madison	Madison	14,692
Yazoo City	Yazoo	14,550
Horn Lake	DeSoto	14,099
Corinth	Alcorn	14,054
Cleveland	Bolivar	13,841
McComb	Pike	13,337
Canton	Madison	12,911
West Point	Clay	12,145
Indianola	Sunflower	12,066
Oxford	Lafayette	11,756
Gautier	Jackson	11,681
Picayune	Pearl River	10,535

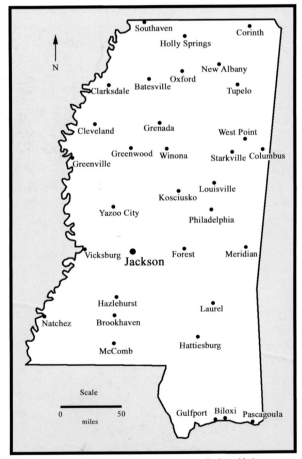

Major Mississippi Municipalities

1

The Original Mississippians

Pre-History

By the time the first Europeans set foot in the region that would become the state of Mississippi, the land had been inhabited for thousands of years. Scholars differ on when the first human beings came into North America, but evidence indicates that a series of migrations from Asia began at least 25,000 years ago, and probably much earlier. The first immigrants followed animals into the continent, crossing an ancient land bridge over the Bering Strait into what is now Alaska. Year after year, decade after decade, century after century, these nomadic peoples fanned out steadily to the south, reaching the tip of South America around 9000 BCE. By the time Christopher Columbus "discovered" the New World in 1492, at least 50 million people lived in the Americas, with as many as 10 million of those residing in the territory that would become the United States.

Small, nomadic bands of humans first reached present-day Mississippi around 10,000 BCE. The region's mild climate was conducive to human habitation, with numerous streams and rivers framing fertile valleys and thick forests. These earliest Mississippians maintained a primitive existence. They used crude stone tools and continually moved around from place to place, always on the hunt. During what archeologists refer to as the Archaic Period (c. 8000 BCE to 1800 BCE), prehistoric cultures in Mississippi became better defined, less nomadic, and more regionalized. The native population continued to hunt, but they also supplemented their food supply with roots, nuts, berries, seeds, and, where available, freshwater and saltwater shellfish. By the end of the Archaic Period the native existence was considerably more stable. More and more they relied on subsistence agriculture, which allowed

Winterville Mounds

The Winterville Mounds, located in the Mississippi Delta near Greenville, were once part of a large prehistoric center of activity built by native inhabitants of the region between 1000 and 1450 CE. The site originally contained at least twenty-three mounds, the largest of which was more than fifty feet high. Archeological evidence indicates that the Native Americans who used the Winterville Mounds had a civilization similar to that of the Natchez Indians, with an elaborate leadership system and layered religious and social structures. The mounds were used for more than four hundred years, but the area's Native American population began to decline during the late 1300s, and by 1450 the mounds had been abandoned. Today the Mississippi Department of Archives and History administers the impressive, forty-two-acre Winterville Mounds site. It is open daily to the public and includes walking trails and a museum housing a variety of Native American artifacts and exhibits.

the population to take full advantage of available plant and animal resources. Large, permanent towns developed, as did networks of trade that spanned the southeast and beyond. Native American settlements maintained their own social and political structures, which became more pronounced over time.

During the Woodland Period (c. 1800 BCE to 1000 CE) the human population of what would become the state of Mississippi increased, and these early inhabitants began producing ceramic pottery and cultivating food staples including corn, squash, and beans. The Woodland Period also saw the introduction of ceremonial mound building in Mississippi. Constructed one basketful of dirt at a time, these earthworks varied in shape, size, and function. Native American societies buried their dead in the mounds, built temples atop them, and worshipped around them. Some mounds stood alone, while others were arranged in groups. They were formidable territorial markers as well as monuments to social and cultural unity. To some, they were sacred symbols of Mother Earth. Through the centuries these mounds retained great meaning for those who built them and those who lived their lives around them. Mound building declined during the late Woodland Period but later experienced a resurgence during the Mississippian Period (c. 1000 to 1700 CE). Today they remain the most visible evidence of Mississippi's ancient Native American heritage.

MISSISSIPPI TRIBES

By the time of European intrusion Mississippi was home to three primary Native American groups: the Choctaws, the Chickasaws, and the Natchez. Smaller tribes also lived in the region, including the Acolapissa, Biloxi, and Pascagoula on the Gulf Coast, and the Ofagoula, Taposa, Yazoo, and Tunica in the Delta. By the mid-1500s the Choctaws were the largest tribe, with around 20,000 members and occupying much of central Mississippi. The Chickasaws, with around 5,000 members, lived in northern Mississippi, while the Natchez, numbering around 4,500, occupied the southwestern part of the state along the Mississippi River.

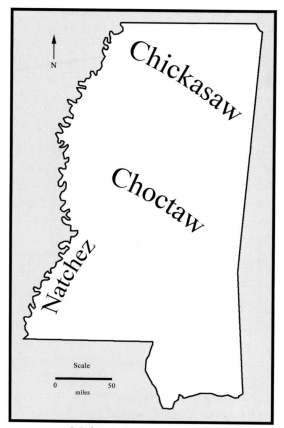

Major Mississippi Tribes

The major Mississippi tribes had many traits in common, although the Natchez were distinct in a number of critical ways. All three shared a common ancestral language, Muskhogean. The Choctaw and Chickasaw languages were almost identical, while the Natchez spoke a variant of the Muskhogean tongue. All the tribes held their land communally, believing that, as with other natural resources, land was meant to provide benefits for the group rather than the individual. They were farmers who grew a variety of crops including corn, beans, squash, pumpkins, and watermelons. The men also hunted deer, bear, turkey, squirrel, and quail. Members of all three tribes lived in towns and constructed their individual houses out of wooden poles, tree branches, woven grass mats, and clay. A council of elders governed each town, and the towns were allied together as a nation. A national council and principle chief or chiefs in turn governed the nation. Most decisions directly affecting tribal life, however, were made at the local level, with the national council serving a more general function to protect the common interest of the nation as a whole.

Within the Choctaw and Chickasaw groups, members enjoyed a relatively wide latitude of individual freedom. The Natchez, however, were ruled by a despotic tribal government, led by a tyrannical chief and privileged class. The social structures and religious practices of the Natchez distinguished them from the other two tribal groups. In general, religion dominated the lives of the Natchez to a greater degree than that of the other tribes. The Natchez believed in a supreme spirit who lived inside the sun, or as they referred to it, the Great Fire. According to legend the Great Spirit had sent a messenger to earth, where he taught the Natchez their religious practices and explained to them how they should govern themselves. Inside their tribal temple, which was built on top of a ten-foot mound, a flame representing the sun burned constantly. The primary Natchez chief, called the Great Sun, ruled the tribe with an iron fist and was believed to be a descendant of the spirit that resided in the sun. Upon his death, relatives, servants, or even volunteers were executed to accompany the chief on his journey into the afterlife.

The Natchez social structure was divided into two distinct classes, the Nobility and the Stinkards. Among the nobility there were three subdivisions: the Sun class, the Nobles, and the honored persons. The Sun class had the highest rank, ruled individual towns, and advised the Great Sun, while the Nobles and Honored Persons were war chiefs and secondary officials. The Stinkards were the commoners of the tribe, and they provided most of the tribe's labor force. While social status among the Natchez was hereditary, members of the Nobility were not forbidden to marry below their station.

The Choctaws and Chickasaws practiced their own religions. Both tribes believed in a great spirit and other minor deities. The Chickasaws' supreme being was a "Beloved One Who Dwells in the Blue Sky," who made his presence known through the sun, lightning, storms, or other natural forces. The Choctaws' primary deity was the sun, which they viewed as a spiritual being whose earthly manifestation was fire. Both tribes believed in life after death, but their burial practices differed. The Choctaws disposed of their deceased tribesmen above

The Grand Village of the Natchez

The Natchez Indians inhabited what is now southwestern Mississippi for hundreds of years before war with the French in 1730 destroyed the tribe. The Natchez culture was at its zenith during the sixteenth century, and between 1682 and 1730 what the French described as "the Grand Village of the Natchez Indians" was the tribe's primary ceremonial center. Throughout the period French explorers, priests, and journalists described the impressive settlement built by the Natchez on the banks of St. Catherine Creek. The heart of the Grand Village was the Temple Mound, on which rested a religious structure that housed a perpetual flame and the bones of previous chiefs. As with the Winterville Mounds one hundred and fifty miles to the north, the Mississippi Department of Archives and History currently administers the Grand Village of the Natchez Indians. In addition to a museum, the 128-acre site includes a reconstructed Natchez Indian house based on historical descriptions, archeo-logical remains, and nature trails. The site also plays host to community events as well as educational programs for adults and children. The Grand Village of the Natchez, located in the present-day city of Natchez, is open daily to the public.

Nanih Waiya

Located 25 miles north of Philadelphia in Winston County, Nanih Waiya mound was once a center of Native American culture, and it remains an integral part of Choctaw tribal heritage today. The structure is a large rectangular platform mound measuring 25 feet high, 218 feet long, and 140 feet wide. Archeologists disagree over the date that the mound was constructed. While its form is typical of mounds built in the region between 1,500 and 2,000 years ago, pottery fragments found in the area suggest that Nanih Waiya may have been built between 100 BCE and 400 CE.

ground, placing the body on a raised platform where it decayed and, in so doing, offered its spiritual essence back to the sun. Chickasaws buried their dead in the floor of the household of the deceased. The body was interred in a sitting position facing west so that the spirit could find its way to the land of the hereafter.

The social structures of the Choctaws and Chickasaws were far less rigid than that of the Natchez. There were few rules, and in general their societies were more democratic. Villages elected their own chiefs, and while national council meetings were held on occasion, the tribes were dedicated to local autonomy. Perhaps because of differences in population size, the Chickasaws had a single major chief for the whole tribe while the Choctaws divided their territory into three districts, each with its own leader. Of the three major Mississippi tribes, the Chickasaws were the more warlike, aggressively defending their homeland from outsiders.

EUROPEAN INTRUSION

The arrival of Europeans in the Mississippi region dramatically altered the Native American cultures in a relatively short period of time. Within fifty years of initial contact, European technology, diseases, politics, and military conflicts fundamentally changed the Native American existence. Within another century the cultures were almost destroyed. By the end of the seventeenth century British traders had reached the Chickasaws in northeastern Mississippi, just as the French were in the process of establishing a colony on the Gulf Coast. The

Europeans brought trade goods with them—cloth, guns, powder, knives, and hatchets—which they exchanged for pelts, particularly deerskins. As the British and French struggled for commercial and political control of the region, the Indians became increasingly dependent on European consumer goods, thus altering their traditional self-sufficient lifestyle.

The Europeans also traded with the Indians for slaves who had been captured during various conflicts. This practice led to the virtual extinction of many of the smaller Native American groups. The larger tribes, particularly the Chickasaws, preyed on their weaker neighbors, raiding villages and seizing every able body. The Chickasaws then sold their captives to the British, who would march them east for sale in the Carolinas. In addition to disrupting the Native American existence through commercial activities, the Europeans also brought diseases with them to which the Indians had no natural immunity. Smallpox, measles, and other illnesses killed off a large segment of the Indian population.

The Natchez were the first of the major Mississippi tribes to feel the full force of European intrusion. By the early eighteenth century the French had established firm trade relationships with the tribe, but in 1714 a trading dispute led to the death of four Frenchmen at the hands of the Indians. As a result, the French increased their military presence in the region and in 1716 constructed Fort Rosalie on the bluffs overlooking the Mississippi River, on the site of the present-day city of Natchez. The presence of the fort encouraged French settlers from the expanding coastal colony to move into the area. With each passing year resentment grew among the Natchez, which led to periodic violence. In 1729 a major Indian uprising claimed the lives of 250 French soldiers and settlers, an event which signaled the end of the Natchez civilization. French troops, with the help of Choctaw mercenaries, retaliated massively, killing and capturing a large number of Natchez and driving the survivors out of the area, where they intermingled with the Chickasaws and smaller tribes. The French sent the Indian prisoners to the West Indies as slaves. By 1731 the Natchez Nation had ceased to exist, leaving the Choctaws and Chickasaws as Mississippi's only major tribes.

As they attempted to gain control of the region, the French and English enlisted Native American allies. The Choctaws were closer to the French, with whom they had established good trade relationships in the south. Likewise, English traders in the north had cultivated the Chickasaws. These loose alliances drew the Mississippi Indians into conflict with each other, and with the Europeans. The Chickasaws, in particular, maintained their reputation as fierce warriors in a series of battles against the French. The first major French–Chickasaw conflict began in 1720 after the tribe refused to banish British traders from its villages. The French first sent Choctaw mercenaries into the north, promising a bounty of one gun, one pound of gunpowder, and two pounds of bullets for each Chickasaw scalp. In response the Chickasaws raided Choctaw villages and attacked French shipping on the Mississippi, virtually closing the river to French traffic for almost four years. Eventually the French recalled the Choctaws and brokered an uneasy peace in 1725. Several years later similar efforts to force the Chickasaws to expel British traders had similar results. In 1736 the French, with their Choctaw allies, again moved north into Chickasaw territory where they suffered a major defeat in northeastern Mississippi at the Battle of Ackia. Subsequent attempts to dislodge the Chickasaws in 1739 and 1752 were unsuccessful, ending French attempts to establish dominance in northern Mississippi.

With the end of the French and Indian War in 1763, the British took control of the region that would become the state of Mississippi. By the time British domination began, significant changes had taken place among the Mississippi Indians. Ancient tribal ways had been corrupted by European intrusion, and disease had killed off a great deal of the population. Smaller tribes had either been wiped out or absorbed by the Choctaws and Chickasaws. In addition, an increase in the mixed-blood population gradually eroded the old forms of tribal government. After decades of interaction with Europeans, the priorities of tribal life had shifted from communal concerns to an emphasis on individual pursuits through trade and other forms of what the intruding Europeans referred to generally as "civilized" conduct. Self-sufficiency gave way to a dependence on European goods that altered

Greenwood Leflore

The son of a French Canadian trader and a mixed-blood Choctaw woman, Greenwood Leflore (1800–1865) was an influential yet controversial Choctaw leader. He was the great nephew of the famous Choctaw chief Pushmataha, and in 1826 he himself became chief of one of the tribe's districts in Mississippi. Leflore believed that Indian life as he knew it was coming to an end and that the Choctaws should make a concerted effort to accept many of the white man's ways. In 1830 he took part in negotiations with the Americans that led to the Treaty of Dancing Rabbit Creek, which ceded the Choctaw lands in Mississippi to the United States. Leflore backed the treaty, although he insisted on a stipulation that allowed individual Choctaw families to remain in Mississippi if they so chose. After the treaty was signed, most of the Choctaws were forced to move from their ancestral homeland to Oklahoma. However, Leflore remained in Mississippi. In return for his cooperation with the United States authorities he received 2,500 prime acres in the Mississippi Delta. He entered white society and became one of the wealthiest men in the state, building up a plantation of 15,000 acres, on which more than 400 slaves toiled daily. From 1840 to 1844 he served in the Mississippi Senate and in 1860 opposed secession. He remained loyal to the United States until his death in 1865. Leflore County was named for him, as was the city of Greenwood. Still, Leflore's affluence led critics to charge that he had sold out his people for personal wealth, and even today many Choctaws consider him a traitor.

not only the Indians' economy, but their ancient social, religious, and political systems as well. Christian missionaries moved among the Native Americans seeking converts and disparaging traditional religious practices as evil. As European encroachment increased, tribal leadership positions were increasingly filled by mixed-blood tribesmen who were more aggressive than their full-blood counterparts and who, it was assumed, could better deal with the whites. For example, Greenwood Leflore, the son of a French trapper and an Indian woman, became a principal Choctaw chief while James Logan Colbert, a Scot, fathered sons who were dominant spokesmen for the Chickasaws for years.

During the period of British rule the Mississippi tribes were relatively peaceful in their dealings with one another and with the whites. They concentrated on trade, and some acted as economic emissaries between the British on the eastern side of the Mississippi River and the Spanish in Louisiana. The outbreak of the American Revolution broke the calm. During the war the Choctaws remained essentially neutral due to the presence of the Spanish in the area (Spain entered the war against the British, capturing Natchez and other British outposts along the Gulf of Mexico). The Chickasaws, however, sided with their old allies against the Americans and became the main British line of defense for the area along the Mississippi up to the Ohio River. Resistance by the Chickasaws, who were supplied with weapons by the British, effectively checked American plans to invade the region. Once the war ended and the British were no longer a factor in the area, the Mississippi Indians were unsure whether to ally themselves with the Americans, who had gained their independence, or with the Spanish, who would lay disputed claim to parts of Mississippi for years to come.

Despite continued attempts by the Spanish to coerce the tribes into an alliance, in late 1785 the Choctaws and Chickasaws sent representatives to Hopewell, South Carolina to negotiate with American commissioners. The result was the Treaty of Hopewell, which declared the tribes at peace with the United States and "under the protection of the United States of America, and no other sovereign whosoever." Even though the Americans continued to encroach on their tribal lands, the tribes stayed loyal to the United States through the early nineteenth century. Under the leadership of Choctaw chief Pushmataha they refused to join the famous Shawnee chief Tecumseh in his efforts to establish an Indian confederation against the Americans during the War of 1812. Both tribes contributed to Andrew Jackson's victory over the Creek Indians at Horseshoe Bend in March of 1814 and less than a year later a thousand warriors under Pushmataha helped Jackson defeat the British at the Battle of New Orleans.

Pushmataha

Having come of age during a time of great change for his people, Pushmataha established himself during the early nineteenth century as one of the greatest Choctaw chiefs. Respected by his fellow tribesmen and whites alike, he spoke four languages—Choctaw, Spanish, English, and French—and played a major role in Choctaw negotiations with the United States.

During extended hunting trips Pushmataha first gained acclaim as a warrior in battles with the Caddo and Osage Indians west of the Mississippi River. He eventually served as chief of the southern district of the Choctaws and emerged as a preeminent Native American spokesman in the southeastern United States. Fighting with American troops against the Creeks during the War of 1812, Pushmataha earned a commission from the federal government as a brigadier general. After the war he remained loyal to the United States but was still able to serve the Choctaws well during negotiations that resulted in the Treaty of Doak's Stand. He unsuccessfully resisted relocation, but his knowledge of western terrain increased the amount and quality of the land that the Choctaws would receive in the Indian Territory. Pushmataha continued agitating for fair treatment for his people, and in 1824 he traveled to Washington to meet with federal officials. While in the nation's capital he died, and was buried with full military honors in the Congressional Cemetery.

The days of the Choctaws and Chickasaws in Mississippi were numbered, however, despite their cooperation with the Americans. In 1798 the United States created the Mississippi Territory, which at the time included much of the present states of Mississippi and Alabama. As the federal government began to officially administer the territory, more and more settlers moved in and the United States began whittling away the Indian lands. In the end, the Mississippi tribes, outmanned and outgunned, realized that they had to reach some type of accommodation with the Americans who coveted their land. By accepting American gifts and assurances of peace

in the future, the Indians hoped to survive on their
remaining territory and perhaps even benefit through trade
with the whites. As a result, in 1801 federal commissioners
negotiated with the Choctaws the Treaty of Fort Adams,
ceding to the United States more than two million acres in
southwestern Mississippi. In 1805 the Choctaws gave up
over four million more acres in southern Mississippi
through the Treaty of Mount Dexter. The Chickasaws gave
up a small parcel of land along the Tombigbee River
through the Treaty of Fort St. Stephens in 1816. In 1817 the
United States divided the Mississippi Territory, bringing
the western half into the Union as the state of Mississippi.
At the time most of the northern part of the state was
reserved for the Indians, but this didn't stop white settlers
from entering the area. The whites were drawn in by the
land, and they quickly discounted treaties or other
regulations governing the Indian reserves. They saw only
the potential for new homes, new towns, and for prosperity,
and they saw the Indians as an impediment to progress.

Statehood increased the already existing pressure on
the Choctaw and Chickasaw Indians to give up their
remaining lands in Mississippi and relocate west of the
Mississippi River. The United States government dealt with
the Choctaws first, primarily because of their closer
proximity to existing white settlement. In 1818 and 1819
efforts to negotiate treaties with the Choctaws failed, much
to the displeasure of Mississippi's citizenry. Sensing the
need for action, President James Monroe appointed
Andrew Jackson to negotiate with the Choctaws.
Mississippi's political leadership praised the choice,
believing that Jackson was by far the best man for the job.
Jackson feigned concern for the Indians' welfare but in
truth believed that the tribe should be relocated as quickly
as possible, and by force if necessary. In 1820 he traveled to
a spot along the Natchez Trace called Doak's Stand, where
he met with Choctaw leaders. The parlay quickly
degenerated into threats and intimidation that resulted in
the Treaty of Doak's Stand. In succumbing to the treaty, the
Choctaws gave up five million acres of their homeland.

Mississippians celebrated the forced removal of the
Choctaws; many considered Jackson's achievement on par
with his much-lauded victory at the Battle of New Orleans.

Ten years later, with Jackson in the White House, the United States government forced the Choctaws to give up the remainder of their claims through the Treaty of Dancing Rabbit Creek. The Chickasaws too gave up all their lands in northern Mississippi in 1832 through the Treaty of Pontotoc. Over the next two decades most of the Indians were relocated to the Indian Territory in present day Oklahoma. A small group of Choctaws chose to remain in the state, forming the nucleus of the present-day Mississippi Band of Choctaws, who live near Philadelphia, Mississippi.

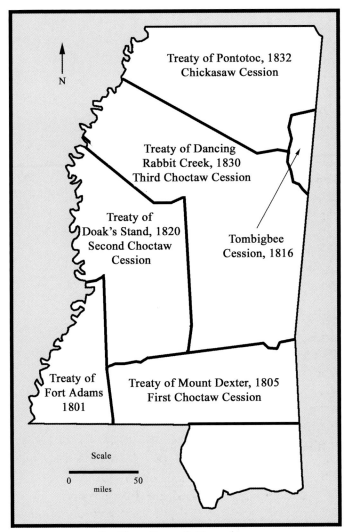

Indian Land Cessions

2

Explorers and Settlers, 1541–1798

I n the late fifteenth century the voyages of Christopher Columbus marked the beginning of a frantic race among the major European powers to spread their influence to the New World. Spain, England, and France all hoped to establish claims in the vast and mysterious new land and plunder its immense riches and apparently limitless raw materials. Like the rest of North America, the land that would become the state of Mississippi became part of this international tug-of-war for global supremacy.

Hernando de Soto

As the Spanish established themselves in South and Central America during the early sixteenth century, they also took the lead in exploring the southeastern corner of the North American mainland. Ponce de Leon and his expedition were the first Europeans to enter the region, claiming Florida for Spain in 1513. In May of 1539 Hernando de Soto, already a veteran of the Spanish conquest of Peru, sailed with a force of 600 men from Havana, Cuba to Florida in search of gold and other riches. The expedition landed near Tampa Bay and marched north along the coast of the Gulf of Mexico. For four years, battling the Native American population much of the way, de Soto and his men explored some 350,000 square miles of what is now the southeastern United States.

De Soto's leadership strained relations between the expedition and the Native Americans to the limit. Wherever he went the arrogant conquistador established a reputation for brutality. His treatment of the various native populations that he encountered was consistently harsh. He made a habit of capturing and holding hostage local chiefs along the way to ensure safe passage through their provinces and, upon his departure, kidnapping and enslaving local tribesmen to carry his expedition's supplies. As he traveled through Florida, Georgia, the Carolinas, Tennessee, and Alabama he pillaged Native American settlements, sometimes robbing burial grounds, and established a general pattern of murder and mayhem. Even those tribes that initially befriended the expedition eventually fell under de Soto's sword. There can be little wonder that as word of the Spanish atrocities spread, de Soto and his men met stronger resistance from various Native American groups. More and more expedition members were lost to ambush, and there were a number of significant skirmishes. During one major battle in Alabama, de Soto's men defeated a significant Native American force but were almost wiped out in the process.

In December of 1540 the expedition crossed into northeastern Mississippi where it soon encountered a large Chickasaw village near the present-day city of Pontotoc. Apparently unaware of de Soto's reputation, the Chickasaws welcomed the Spanish, and for a time, relations between the two camps remained friendly. De Soto and his men spent the winter of 1540–1541 with the tribe, during which time peace prevailed, gifts were exchanged, and the visitors even prepared a feast for their Chickasaw hosts. By March of 1541 the expedition was well rested, well healed, and ready to move out. No longer needing to take advantage of the Native American hospitality, de Soto broke the peace by belligerently demanding from the Chickasaw chief two hundred of his subjects to serve as burden-bearers for the next leg of the expedition's journey. In response the Chickasaws stalled for time and made plans to attack the Spanish camp. Several nights later the Chickasaws ambushed de Soto's men as they slept, and according to one Spanish participant, "a sudden and very cruel nocturnal battle" ensued. The Native Americans used flaming arrows to burn the Spanish huts, stables, and livestock pens. Caught by surprise, de Soto's men scrambled to fend off the assault. After two hours the Spanish managed to drive the Chickasaws away, but the battle was costly. The expedition sustained a number of casualties and lost most of its livestock and supplies. After the battle, de Soto's expedition limped west across northern Mississippi. In May of 1541, near present-day Tunica County, they reached the Mississippi River, crossed over, and continued wandering through Arkansas. Sick and disheartened, de Soto made his way back to the Mississippi River in 1542. In May of that year he died, probably at a site about ten miles south of Helena, Arkansas, and was buried in the great river that he would be credited with "discovering." The expedition, which now numbered less than three hundred, tried unsuccessfully to find an overland route to Mexico. The group returned to the Mississippi, floated down it to the Gulf of Mexico, and eventually arrived in Vera Cruz in September of 1543.

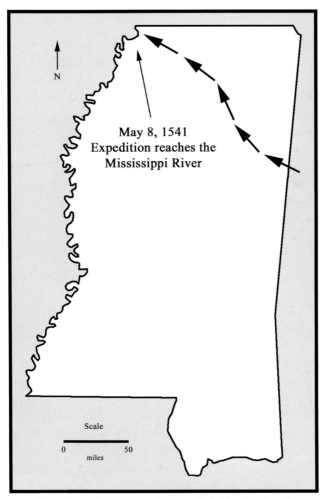

N

May 8, 1541
Expedition reaches the
Mississippi River

Scale

0   50
miles

De Soto's route through Mississippi (approximate)

While Spain never colonized the Mississippi region, de Soto's foray into the southeast did leave a lasting legacy. The Spaniards established a reputation for brutality among the indigenous population by enslaving many of the Native Americans, seizing food stores, and burning villages. A variety of maladies brought to the region by de Soto and his men devastated the Native Americans, who lacked immunity to European diseases. As a result, the populations of the various tribes decreased dramatically in the years after the Spaniards' visit. Although de Soto's expedition raised serious doubts over the presence of gold in the area, thus discouraging further Spanish exploration, this first serious Spanish foray into the American Southeast firmly established the Mississippi region in the geographic consciousness of future European explorers and forever linked de Soto's name with the Mississippi River.

LOUIS JOLIET AND JACQUES MARQUETTE

Little exploration took place in Mississippi for decades after de Soto's expedition as the major European powers were occupied elsewhere. As the struggle for supremacy in the New World continued, however, the Mississippi River Valley and the coastal region along the Gulf of Mexico would once again draw their attention. Although in decline as a world power by the end of the early seventeenth century, Spain was determined to maintain control in Florida and adjacent territories. Meanwhile, France was equally determined to establish itself in the New World. The French settled Quebec in 1608 and began moving slowly west and south on a course that would eventually spread French influence down the Mississippi River. As they did so, the French navy began wresting control of a number of Caribbean Islands from the Spanish. The northern coast of Santo Domingo became a French colony in 1629, followed by the islands of Martinique and Guadalupe six years later. French pirates roamed the high seas, plundering Spanish ships. While the struggle in the Caribbean continued for some time, all parties concerned eventually realized that control of the mainland, along the great river that flowed from deep within the continent, was of the utmost importance.

In the north the French had been interested in exploring the Mississippi River for some time. Rumors concerning the river's course both alarmed and intrigued French authorities. Some claimed that the river followed an eastern course to Virginia, a route that might leave France vulnerable to the English on the Atlantic Coast. Others claimed the river actually flowed into the southwest, and therefore might serve as an invasion route for the French into the Spanish colonies in Mexico. As late as 1670 some held out hope that the river might somehow empty into the Pacific Ocean, providing the long-elusive water route to the Far East. Regardless of these rumors, it was apparent to the French that they needed to expand into the Mississippi Valley, and to do so they first needed to explore the river itself. To this end, the governor of New France chose French-Canadian explorer Louis Joliet to lead an expedition down the Mississippi.

Joliet was born near the city of Quebec in 1645 and was educated for the priesthood in a Jesuit Seminary. After briefly studying in France he abandoned the church, returned to Canada, and established himself as a trader with the Native Americans. He had already explored parts of the region due to his trade and therefore had the experience to lead a major expeditionary force down river. Because it was customary that a priest be part of such an expedition, French missionary Jacques Marquette was chosen to accompany Joliet and serve as chaplain. A Jesuit since he was a teenager, Marquette had come to Canada as a missionary in 1666. He had already mastered several Native American languages and viewed the expedition as a great opportunity to enlist new converts. Besides Joliet and Marquette, five other men made up the group as it left Green Bay on Lake Michigan in May of 1673.

On June 17 the expedition reached the Wisconsin River and then entered the Mississippi. Joliet and Marquette traveled as far south as the mouth of the Arkansas River, which is opposite present-day Rosedale, Mississippi. There, satisfied that the river actually flowed south into the Gulf of Mexico, the expedition turned back. Joliet and Marquette were also concerned that if they moved further south their small party might be vulnerable to attacks from hostile Native American tribes, or possibly from their European rivals. Whether the group actually set foot on Mississippi state soil is unclear, though many historians believe that they probably did. Regardless, the expedition sparked great interest in the Mississippi Valley among the French. Soon others would build on the accomplishments of Joliet and Marquette, retracing their route and eventually following the river all the way to the Gulf of Mexico.

LA SALLE AND TONTY

Joliet and Marquette's return to Canada generated great excitement among French authorities and sparked the imagination of another explorer, René-Robert Cavelier Sieur de La Salle. Born in France in 1643, La Salle, like Joliet, was educated by Jesuits but eventually left the order to make his fortune elsewhere. He immigrated to Canada in 1666 and established himself as a trader in the North American wilderness. His work took him among numerous Native American tribes. He became familiar with a variety of Native American languages and cultures, and would later claim that he discovered the Ohio River. By the late 1670s the ambitious La Salle had made a name for himself in Canada. He had also hatched a well-received plan to descend the Mississippi River to its mouth and establish a major fort and trading post on the Gulf Coast. Through his experience as a trader and his political connections, La Salle received a royal commission for the project. He was given five years to complete the mission at his own expense. In return, he would receive any profits from trade and ownership of any forts that he might establish along the way. For the project La Salle enlisted the aid of his friend Henry de Tonty, son of a prominent Italian family and a favorite of the French monarch. Tonty was probably one of the most colorful characters ever to navigate the Mississippi. As a youth he served in the French army where he lost a hand, which he replaced with an intimidating artificial metal hand. He became a legendary figure among the Native American tribes as he explored North America, in large part because they believed that the artificial hand had magical powers. As a result, Tonty was one of La Salle's chief assets on the expedition.

La Salle and Tonty set out in August of 1681 with an expedition that included a Franciscan father, twenty-three other Frenchmen, eighteen Native American men, ten Native American women, and three children. They reached the river on February 2, 1682, and by the end of the month the group was camped at Chickasaw Bluffs, near present-day Memphis, where they enjoyed friendly relations with the local tribes. In early April the expedition reached the mouth of the Mississippi. There La Salle planted a cross and claimed the entire area drained by the river (technically a vast area from the Appalachian Mountains to the Rocky Mountains) for France, naming it "Louisiana" in honor of King Louis XIV. Though his enthusiasm never waned, La Salle did not realize his dream of establishing a major French fort at the mouth of the Mississippi. After the expedition he returned to Canada and then, leaving Tonty behind, left for France, where he appealed to the king for more men and supplies. Impressed with La Salle's discovery, the king named him Viceroy of North America and approved another expedition that would approach the mouth of the river from the Gulf of Mexico. In 1684 La Salle left France with four ships and four hundred men who would serve as an occupying force once the new fort was established, but the ships missed their target. The expedition ended up landing on the Texas coast, where it endured great hardships. La Salle's men eventually revolted and murdered their leader. Tonty, who had not accompanied La Salle on this new endeavor, continued traveling the Mississippi and remained involved in the French effort to colonize North America.

FRENCH SETTLEMENT

Any efforts to colonize the Mississippi Valley were put on hold in 1688 as the major European powers became embroiled in the War of the League of Augsburg. The conflict dragged on for nine years with England and Spain aligned against the French, whose reigning monarch Louis XIV was determined to spread French influence globally. The conflict primarily took place in Europe, but the shadow of North America and the potential for colonial expansion loomed large. The Treaty of Ryswick ended the conflict and ostensibly recognized the general claims that the European powers had in America before the war began, including England's colonies on the Atlantic seaboard, Spanish possessions in Florida and Mexico, and tenuous French claims in the Mississippi Valley and on the Gulf

Coast. In reality the treaty ushered in a new era of colonial rivalry. Temporarily freed from war with one another, the Europeans began to focus their energies on America and the coveted Mississippi Valley. France wanted to hold its claim to the Mississippi Valley, establish a lucrative fur trade in the region, and keep the English confined to the Atlantic Coast. England sought to expand its existing colonies to the west, while the Spanish wanted to bridge the gap between its holdings in Florida and Mexico.

Building on its initial exploration of the area, France took the lead in colonizing parts of what would become the state of Mississippi. Pierre LeMoyne, Sieur d'Iberville, a highly regarded sailor and explorer, was chosen to head the effort. Born in Canada into a prominent French military family, Iberville was appointed a midshipman in the French navy in 1675 at the age of fourteen. He made a name for himself fighting the British, and in 1698 the French government commissioned him to colonize the mouth of the Mississippi River. Iberville procured two frigates and two smaller ships, which he loaded with supplies, soldiers, and colonists. The expedition set out from France in October of 1698. Iberville sailed first to Santo Domingo, where he picked up more supplies, and then moved toward the North American mainland. The expedition reached the coast of Florida, near the mouth of the Apalachicola River, and then sailed to the west. When Iberville found that the Spanish already occupied Pensacola Bay, and that Mobile Bay was too shallow to enter, he moved on to the Mississippi Coast. There he discovered and named Ship Island (for its silhouette on the horizon) and Cat Island (for its large population of raccoons that the French mistook for cats), which were several miles from the mainland. After anchoring off Ship Island, Iberville dispatched a landing party to the mainland, where they entered a bay and encountered local Native Americans who were members of the Biloxi tribe. The Native Americans fled when the party approached, but eventually the French established friendly relations with the local inhabitants. Iberville named the bay Biloxi, after the tribe.

While his expedition was safe, Iberville was still not convinced that he was near the mouth of the great river that La Salle had described twenty years earlier. Armed with information provided by the Biloxi, he loaded part of his expedition into his smaller boats and sailed west. The group located the river, and sailed up it in search of proof that it was indeed the Mississippi. After traveling almost 300 miles in ten days, the group encountered Native Americans who had in their possession a letter and prayer book left by Henry de Tonty during a search for La Salle's second, ill fated expedition. This proved to Iberville that he was indeed on the Mississippi and the expedition returned to Ship Island. Iberville initially planned to establish a settlement closer to the river, but,

Ocean Springs

First settled by the French in 1699, Ocean Springs is one of America's oldest cities. Pierre LeMoyne d'Iberville and members of his expedition were the first Europeans to set foot in Mississippi, claiming the region for their king and constructing Fort Maurepas where Ocean Springs stands today. The Gulf Coast settlement was the first capital of France's Louisiana colony and a base of operations from which the French expanded their holdings. A reproduction of Fort Maurepas now stands near the beach about a mile away from the original landing site, and each year Ocean Springs recreates Iberville's landing as part of a festival celebrating the area's heritage.

running short on supplies, he decided instead to build a fort on the eastern bank of Biloxi Bay, which is the site of present-day Ocean Springs. The French built a four-sided wooden palisade, with a bastion at each corner, and Iberville christened the structure Fort Maurepas. It was the Louisiana colony's first settlement, and the first European settlement in what would become the state of Mississippi.

While Fort Maurepas established a French foothold in the region, the settlement itself was short-lived. After seeing the fort constructed, Iberville returned to France, leaving behind his friend Sauvole de la Villantry to command a garrison of around eighty men. Iberville's younger brother, Jean Baptiste Le Moyne, Sieur de Bienville, also remained at Biloxi Bay to serve as Sauvole's chief lieutenant. When Sauvole died from fever in 1701, Bienville was left in charge of the colony. The French struggled for the next several years to make the colony profitable, but in 1702 they abandoned Fort Maurepas in favor of a new, more strategically desirable site to the east on Mobile Bay.

Iberville periodically shuttled to and from France to secure funds and recruit settlers, while Bienville led expeditions that explored the region and established relatively friendly relations with the local Native Americans. Despite these efforts, however, the colony failed to prosper. Food production was a constant problem. The coastal soil was ill-suited for growing European food crops, and attempts to grow Indian crops met with only mixed success. Word of the colony's harsh existence filtered back to France, hampering the recruitment of settlers. The population of the colony remained primarily male, and while French authorities brought some women to Louisiana, a family-oriented settlement so crucial to permanent colonization never completely took hold.

Private Administration

Louisiana struggled as a royal colony from 1699 to 1712. Fighting between France and Britain isolated the region for years at a time during the early 1700s, and the colony remained a financial burden on the French treasury. Hoping to curtail expenses and encourage private investment, the French crown finally offered a charter for the private administration of the colony, and in 1712 wealthy financier Antoine Crozat received permission to operate Louisiana for fifteen years. While Crozat had high hopes that he could improve the colony's dismal financial condition, he abandoned the venture after five years, having exhausted much of his resources without realizing a return. The population of the colony remained small, with only a few hundred colonists living a tenuous existence at best. Most of the area's interior remained unexplored. One of the few significant events that took place during Crozat's tenure was the establishment of Fort Rosalie on the Mississippi River at the site of present-day Natchez.

In 1717 the rights to the slowly developing Louisiana colony passed to the Mississippi Company, which was organized by Scottish financier John Law. The energetic Law had helped establish the French national bank and, in the process, had gained significant influence in the court of Louis XIV. The bank invested heavily in Law's scheme to the point that the Louisiana project became the bank's primary asset. Using an aggressive marketing campaign, Law set out to develop the colony as quickly as possible. He promised investors in the venture a quick return and assured potential French settlers that a paradise lay across the Atlantic along the Gulf of Mexico. Initially investors flocked to the project, as did settlers, but Mississippi had been oversold, and as a result the stock in the company was significantly overvalued. Despite growth in the population of the colony, the promised profits never materialized and "the Mississippi Bubble," as it came to be known, burst in 1720. The company's stock prices collapsed, stockholders lost their investments, and Law fled from France a ruined man. Ironically, while Law's financial scheme failed miserably, his salesmanship had brought enough settlers to the region to guarantee the colony's survival. The Mississippi Company continued to administer the colony for the next several years, and by 1728 Louisiana had a population of 4,300, including 1,800 slaves, scattered along the coast and at Fort Rosalie on the Mississippi River.

Old Spanish Fort

Around 1718 early French settler Joseph Simon de la Pointe built what is now known as the Old Spanish Fort (a misnomer), around which the Gulf Coast city of Pascagoula grew up. The structure is the oldest building in the Mississippi Valley, featuring 18-inch-thick walls made of oyster shells, moss, and mud. The fort originally included two rooms, with a third room added around 1820. A museum on the grounds now contains Native American artifacts from the area as well as relics from eighteenth century European settlement. Both the museum and the renovated building are open to the public.

Slavery in the Louisiana Colony

The use of slave labor in Louisiana helped the colony survive by producing a nominal amount of agricultural exports, primarily low-grade tobacco, rice, indigo, and silk. Slavery had been part of the colony almost since its creation, but most slaves were not of local origin. The French had tried to enslave local natives, but this yielded little success because the Indians were susceptible to European diseases and could easily escape into the region's interior. Although many of the colony's settlers arrived in the New World as indentured servants, they too did not satisfy the need for a long-term, large-scale labor effort. So, like their English rivals on the eastern seaboard, the French turned to importing African slaves to satisfy their labor needs. Skin color and language isolated the Africans in the New World, and they could not escape to the interior and blend in with the Native American tribes. Because of their homeland's relative proximity to Europe, imported Africans also had greater resistance to European diseases. By the early 1720s the slave population had grown to such an extent that French colonial leaders took steps to strictly regulate slave activity and further define the relationship between blacks and whites in the colony. Bienville, who had again assumed the office of colonial governor, drew up a set of laws called "Black Codes." The central elements of the codes forbade slaves to own land, congregate without white supervision, and "carry offensive weapons or heavy sticks." Punishment for slaves who violated these edicts ranged from whipping and branding to, in extreme cases, death. Some of the French laws restricting slave activity mirrored those that would be established by legislatures in the southern United States during the antebellum period. Bienville's codes also made provisions for elderly or incapacitated slaves and directed all masters to provide Catholic instruction for their servants.

British Dominion

In 1763 the end of the French and Indian War (1754–1763) dashed French dreams of a colonial empire in the Mississippi Valley. As part of the peace settlement, the British received all Spanish claims in Florida as well as all of the French holdings east of the Mississippi River, with the exception of New Orleans. Spain retained New Orleans and territory west of the Mississippi. Thus the region that would one day become the state of Mississippi came under British rule. The British organized part of the region as the Province of West Florida. Once West Florida was organized, many of the area's French residents moved west across the Mississippi to escape British authority. The British set West Florida's official boundaries as the Mississippi River in the west, the Chattahoochee River in the east, and the Gulf of Mexico in the south. The northern boundary was set at 32° 30' latitude, along a line stretching east from a point near present-day Vicksburg. The British reserved the area north of the line for Native Americans by proclamation in 1763. Settlement in the reserved area by whites was forbidden without the permission of the Native American inhabitants.

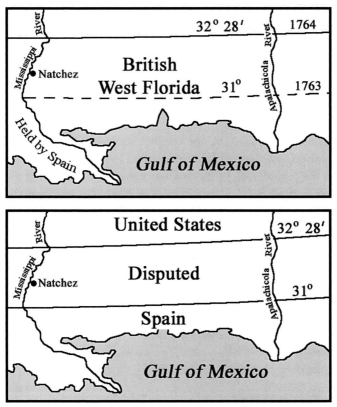

Mississippi Region after Treaties of Paris 1763 (top) and 1783

The British moved slowly to occupy the old Louisiana colony, first taking control of the existing coastal settlements and then moving north. They soon rebuilt Fort Rosalie on the Mississippi River, which had been all but abandoned since the Natchez attacked it in 1729, and renamed it Fort Panmure. The fort soon became a magnet for British settlement. Spurred by news of fertile soil along the Mississippi, settlers, adventurers, and land speculators began trickling into West Florida. The population of the settlement rose as the British government began issuing free land to veterans of the French and Indian War. Many settlers came from the Carolinas, Georgia, and Virginia. In 1772 Amos Ogden, a naval officer, received a large land grant and, along with two partners, established the "Jersey Settlement," so named because many of its residents hailed originally from New Jersey. Still, West Florida grew slowly, and by the 1770s there were only three significantly populated areas in the colony: land along the Tombigbee River above Mobile, the colonial capital at Pensacola, and the area around Natchez.

THE AMERICAN REVOLUTION

While West Florida was relatively isolated and actual fighting within the region was limited during the American Revolution, the conflict between the American colonies and the British certainly had critical repercussions on the region. One of the greatest immediate impacts of the war was an increase in settlement. Many Tories from the Atlantic seaboard who remained loyal to the British Crown fled persecution by the Americans and sought refuge in the west. The increase in population led to the creation of the town of Natchez in 1776. A year later the Natchez District, a substantial area around the town and along the Mississippi River, was created as an administrative subdivision of the region.

West Florida remained peaceful during the first three years of the war, but eventually fighting broke out between Spanish and British forces. Across the Mississippi River from West Florida lay the remainder of the old Louisiana colony, which had been governed by Spain since the end of the French and Indian War half a century earlier. As the American Revolution engulfed the governments of the

King's Tavern

Built prior to 1789, King's Tavern is thought to be the oldest building in Natchez. It was constructed using cypress planks, sun-baked bricks, and large ships' timbers, and dates from the city's Spanish period. The old tavern was a social center in Natchez. When the first United States mail was brought to the city by Indian courier, it was distributed from a small post office on the building's first floor. According to legend the tavern is haunted by the ghost of a serving girl named Madeline, who was the mistress of tavern owner, Richard King. When King's wife found out about her husband's dalliance, she supposedly had Madeline killed and bricked into the fireplace of the main dining room. During the 1930s three skeletons were found buried in the tavern, giving rise to more ghost stories and speculation about the building's past. Today, the restored tavern is a popular a bar and restaurant.

Photo of King's Tavern taken on March 29, 1934 by Ralph Clynne. Courtesy of the Library of Congress.

civilized world, ancient European rivalries came into play. In 1779 Spain entered the war against Britain. With most British forces occupied elsewhere, the Spanish moved across the Mississippi River and captured major settlements in West Florida, including Natchez, Baton Rouge, Mobile, and Pensacola. In 1781 Spain officially took administration of the region.

At the end of the American Revolution, Britain signed separate treaties with Spain and the United States. The British treaty with the Americans fixed the southern boundary of the United States at the thirty-first parallel, the southern border between the present-day states of Mississippi and Louisiana. It also gave the Americans full access to the Mississippi River. However, the British treaty with Spain stated that because Spain had conquered West Florida during the war, Great Britain had no right to cede the land to another nation through treaty. As a result, Spain claimed the region that would include much of the state of Mississippi, and as Spanish military forces occupied the area, the fledgling United States could do little to assert its own claims. To confuse matters further, the state of Georgia also staked an independent claim to the region for a time.

The Spanish did their best to maintain control. They closed the Mississippi to American shipping and encouraged additional settlement of the region in hopes that if necessary, the area's residents would resist against any encroachment by the United States. The Spanish also entered into a conspiracy with James Wilkinson, a former general in the American army during the Revolution and a successful Kentucky businessman. According to the plan, Wilkinson would take the lead in persuading western settlers to break away from the United States and join Spain. The plot involved liberal land grants and duty-free shipping permits that the former general would disperse to key western leaders. In the end, however, the conspiracy failed. Westerners had little interest in an open rebellion against the United States, and Spain's further decline as a world power rendered the effort untenable. The Spanish finally gave up claims in Mississippi north of the 31st parallel in 1795 through the Treaty of San Lorenzo. They would not abandon the coastal region for several years to come, but the treaty paved the way for the United States government to create the Mississippi Territory.

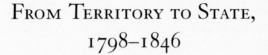

3

FROM TERRITORY TO STATE,
1798–1846

THE MISSISSIPPI TERRITORY

The United States officially created the Mississippi Territory on April 7, 1798. The new territory was bounded on the north by a line drawn east from the mouth of the Yazoo River, on the south by the 31st parallel, on the west by the Mississippi River, and on the east by the Chattahoochee River, which now forms part of the eastern border of Alabama. Land above the northern boundary was reserved for Native Americans. President John Adams appointed Winthrop Sargent of Massachusetts as Mississippi's first territorial governor. After arriving in Mississippi, Sargent created a rudimentary territorial government from scratch with a court system and a militia. He also divided the territory into districts with a sheriff, justice of the peace, and other officers. Natchez, the region's most significant settlement, became the first territorial capital. Sargent ruled the territory with an iron fist and used his power to increase his considerable wealth. In addition to instituting a territorial government, he created laws under which he received large fees for marriage licenses and tavern licenses, along with his share of other public monies. Because of his relentless self promotion, Sargent made enemies within the political sphere. His main opponents were Anthony Hutchins and Cato West, both of whom consistently wrote to the United States Congress with complaints about Sargent's administration.

In 1800 the national presidential election led to a change in the government of the Mississippi Territory. That year Republican Thomas Jefferson won the presidency over Federalist John Adams. Soon after taking office, Jefferson dismissed Sargent from his post and appointed fellow

Republican William C. C. Claiborne as territorial governor, a post which he held until 1805. During Claiborne's tenure he settled old land claims, created new counties, and presided over significant territorial growth. In 1802, as a result of the change in administrations, the territorial capital was moved six miles west of Natchez, which was perceived as a Federalist stronghold, to Washington, Mississippi, a town presumably friendlier to Republicans.

In the interim between the creation of the territory in 1798 and statehood in 1817, most of Mississippi remained a wilderness. With the exception of Natchez, there were no significant towns in the territory and many new settlers to the region had to struggle just to survive. Despite the inhospitable environment, however, there were signs of growth. In 1801 the United States negotiated a treaty with the Choctaws and Chickasaws to build a road across their land. This road eventually stretched from Natchez to Nashville (about 450 miles) and became known as the Natchez Trace. It was really little more than a collection of Indian trails that had been widened and somewhat better defined by the government. Even though it was crude, the road was heavily traveled for years, particularly by people heading north. Boatmen who

Mason and Harpe

Because it was well traveled but largely unpoliced, the Natchez Trace attracted outlaws. The most notorious gang of highwaymen that operated on the Trace during the peak years of the early nineteenth century was the Mason-Harpe gang. Led by Samuel Mason and Wiley Harpe, the gang terrorized the Trace for several years, robbing and killing scores of travelers. Finally, territorial governor William C. C. Claiborne posted a $2,000 reward for the gang's capture. This was a great deal of money at the time, and as the story goes, when Harpe heard about the reward he left the gang, fled north, and disappeared into Kentucky. After Harpe's departure, Mason kept the gang together and gained even greater notoriety along the Trace. Two members of the gang eventually turned on Mason, hoping to collect the reward themselves. They killed their leader, cut off his head, and took it to the authorities as proof that they had indeed ended the career of the notorious outlaw. Unfortunately for the two men, someone that they had robbed in the past recognized them as part of the gang, and the criminals were jailed and eventually hanged for their crimes.

had brought cargo down the Mississippi River to Natchez or New Orleans would travel the Trace back to Nashville, connecting there with other roads. It was a long trip, but it was much easier than fighting the current of the Mississippi back upstream. The Natchez Trace remained a vital overland route for roughly a quarter of a century, but its fate as a major transportation artery was sealed with the invention of the

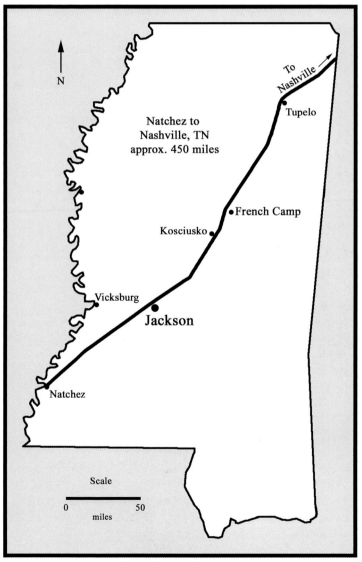

Natchez Trace

steamboat, which made travel upriver much easier. By 1821 there were sixty-one steamboats operating on the Mississippi and Ohio Rivers, and by 1830 the Trace was being used primarily for local travel. Unused portions of the road soon reverted back to wilderness.

Additional lands were annexed to the original Mississippi Territory in 1805 and 1810. Because the territory had changed hands so many times in a relatively short period, there was lingering confusion about the precise claims to territorial lands. Even though the Spanish had relinquished their claims to land north of the 31st parallel, Georgia continued to press some of its claims in the region. In 1802 the United States paid Georgia more than $1.25 million to settle the dispute, and two years later a vast area extending north to the Tennessee state line was added to the Mississippi Territory. This annexation more than doubled the size of the territory, though most of the land in question was reserved for Native Americans for many years. The final addition to the Mississippi Territory took place between 1810 and 1813

William Dunbar

A Scotsman by birth who was educated at King's College in Aberdeen, William Dunbar came to America in 1771 at the age of twenty-one. He arrived in Philadelphia and later made his way south, first to Baton Rouge and finally to Natchez. There he established a large plantation as well as a reputation as a brilliant scientist and one of the leading minds of the Mississippi Territory. Dunbar studied astronomy, chemistry, biology, the weather, and anything else that he deemed worthy of investigation. He applied his knowledge of science and mechanics to produce a number of inventions, including a screw press that would introduce square cotton bales as the primary method for packaging cotton. In 1798 he became surveyor general of the Natchez region and a year later made the first meteorological observations of the Mississippi Valley.

In 1804 Thomas Jefferson appointed Dunbar and Dr. George Hunter to head an exploratory expedition into the Louisiana Purchase. The Hunter-Dunbar expedition eventually traveled up the Ouachita River to a site near present-day Hot Springs, Arkansas. In his journals Dunbar made reports on Indian sign language, native animals and plants, fossils, and astronomical phenomena in the region. His observations were later published in *Documents Relating to the Purchase and Exploration of Louisiana* (1904). Dunbar belonged to the American Philosophical Society, and near the end of his life he became a judge and member of the territorial legislature in Mississippi. Until his death in 1810, he continued performing scientific experiments on his plantation.

when Spain, lacking adequate resources to maintain control of the area, finally yielded its holdings along the Gulf Coast. The result was an expanse that would eventually become parts of Alabama and Mississippi.

THE BURR CONSPIRACY

The Mississippi Territory played host to a bit of national intrigue in 1807 as former vice-president Aaron Burr made his way down the Mississippi River to Natchez. Burr had served as attorney general of New York and as a US senator during the late eighteenth century and was one of the most controversial political figures of his time. As vice-president under Thomas Jefferson, Burr forfeited much of his influence because he often clashed with the president. He permanently sealed his political fate in 1804 when he killed Alexander Hamilton in a highly publicized duel. Three years later Burr became involved in a scheme that he mistakenly believed would result in his political comeback, but in fact his involvement actually ended any hope for his political recovery. Even though the exact nature of the so-called "Burr Conspiracy" remains shrouded in mystery, certain elements of the scheme have been revealed over time. Burr had purchased land across the Mississippi River in the newly acquired Louisiana Territory and apparently planned to seize more land in the southwest. Some believe that he aspired to build his own republic in the region, with the help of the Spanish. The American soldier James Wilkinson, who had conspired with Spain to wrest the territory away from the United States, was at one point Burr's close associate in the project, but eventually he turned on the former vice-president. Burr was arrested and tried for treason before the Mississippi Territorial Court, but the charges were eventually dropped for lack of evidence. Later Burr was again indicted for treason, but he was acquitted after a six-month trial in Richmond, Virginia.

THE WAR OF 1812

During the War of 1812 the eastern portion of the Mississippi Territory—the area that would eventually become the state of Alabama—saw some fighting, primarily between the United States and the Creek Indians, who had aligned themselves with the British. Many Mississippians contributed to the war effort. Ferdinand Claiborne, brother of William C. C. Claiborne, organized and led a Mississippi militia into the eastern part of the territory to aid an army of Tennessee militiamen, led by future president Andrew Jackson, in fighting the Creeks. The major battle that broke the back of the Creek Indians was the Battle of Horseshoe Bend, fought in March of 1814 in present day Tallapoosa County, Alabama. Many Mississippians also took part in the climactic battle of the War of 1812, the Battle of New Orleans, where Jackson commanded the entire American force. The Americans defeated the British at New Orleans in January of 1815, making Jackson a war hero and launching him on a course that would take him to the White House. The battle endeared Jackson to many Mississippians, and throughout his political career Jackson had many admirers in the state.

STATEHOOD

In 1817, Congress divided the Mississippi Territory at the present-day boundary of Mississippi and Alabama. At the time, the western half of the divided territory was deemed ready for statehood with a population of approximately 25,000 whites and 23,000 slaves. On December 10, 1817 James Monroe signed the congressional resolution admitting Mississippi into the Union "on an equal footing with the original states, in all respects whatever." When Mississippi became the nation's twentieth state it was a wilderness, and most of its territory was the domain of the Choctaw and Chickasaw Indians. With the exception of a small area of land east of the Tombigbee River, only the southern part of Mississippi was open for settlement, and the old Natchez District in the southwest along the Mississippi River held most of the state's population, both white and black.

Mississippi's first Constitution was a product of the old Natchez District's conservative leadership. At the Constitutional Convention that drafted the document, delegates from the western counties outnumbered those from the east by two to one—thirty-two to sixteen. In addition, the Piney Woods delegation included the few men of property in the region, men likely to see the benefits of aligning themselves with the Natchez planters when considering major issues. However, even if the Piney Woods delegates had united against the west, they did not have sufficient numbers to carry any proposal through to fruition. As a result, the Mississippi Constitution of 1817 was an undemocratic, conservative document when compared to those drawn up by other western states during the same period. Even though there were only slight restrictions on franchise, there were considerable property and religious qualifications for holding office. Representation in the state senate was based on white taxable population rather than total white population, and almost all state and county officials were legislative appointees. In addition, only significant property owners could hold high elective office. For example, a state senator had to own at least 300 acres of land or other real estate valued at $1,000. To be elected governor a candidate had to own at least 600 acres of land or taxable property worth $2,000. When Mississippi entered the Union in 1817, Natchez became the state's capital.

NATCHEZ AND THE PINEY WOODS

Permanent European settlement in Mississippi first took root in the Natchez District during the early eighteenth century. The region passed through French, British, and Spanish dominion before finally becoming part of the United States. Cotton was cultivated in the district as early as 1721 in soil that was exceedingly fertile. Though on the fringes of a wilderness, the district's location along the river gave Natchez planters easy access to markets, and cotton quickly became the region's primary export. The growth of plantations produced a considerable amount of wealth for a minority of citizens. Activity along the river also allowed pockets of cosmopolitan culture to develop. The city of Natchez eventually became the socio-cultural center of the region. By the beginning of the nineteenth century the settlement had a highly structured government and firmly entrenched political elite. When Mississippi achieved statehood, the Natchez District claimed three quarters of the state's assessed property value along with the state's highest concentration of slaves. The state's political power rested in the hands of a small number of wealthy Natchez

Natchez under the Hill

At the turn of the nineteenth century the city of Natchez was flourishing on a high bluff overlooking the Mississippi River in the southwestern corner of the newly created Mississippi Territory. The Natchez area had been settled for generations and cotton fortunes were in the process of being made there. Though located on the fringes of a wilderness, the city was the cultural center of the Mississippi Territory. The river gave Natchez access to the outside world and conferred a cosmopolitan air to some of the Natchez gentry. As culture made its way up the bluff, however, it first had to pass through the Natchez riverfront, or "Natchez under the Hill," as the area was known throughout the western frontier.

Natchez under the Hill had its own distinct culture. Bawdy rivermen drank in taverns there and patronized houses of ill repute. Gambling and other vices of all kinds were celebrated. For decades the Natchez riverfront generated tales of fierce brawls, murder, intrigue, and larger-than-life characters who passed into legend. The riverboat era increased activity on the riverfront, and at any given time dozens of vessels could be found crowded together along the Natchez docks loaded with cotton. Above the hill on the bluffs the more respectable elements of Natchez society looked down on the riverfront district with a mixture of disdain and curiosity. Today Natchez under the Hill is a popular tourist stop. The sordid taverns and brothels that once attracted rivermen are long gone, replaced by nice restaurants, bars, shops, and, ironically, a legitimate riverboat casino. Tourists move freely along the riverfront shopping, dining, and enjoying the view of the river.

planters who held a decidedly conservative view of events going on around them.

East of Natchez District and across the Pearl River lay the Piney Woods region—land that the Choctaw Indians ceded to the United States in 1805. Poorer farmers, as opposed to more affluent plantation owners, had settled here soon after the War of 1812. They worked soil less fertile then that of the Natchez District, raised livestock, and grew primarily corn and other food crops rather than cotton. Residents of the Natchez District looked down their noses at their eastern neighbors, believing them to be primitive and uncivilized, and, as such, ill suited to contribute to public affairs. The citizens of the Piney Woods, conversely, distrusted the Natchez political hierarchy and chafed under its thumb as they struggled for a voice in state government.

POLITICS AND SECTIONAL RIVALRY

Intra-state section-alism dominated Mississippi politics during the state's early years. Unlike other states, Missi-ssippi was settled from west to east, so the initially dominant western Natchez District had to battle to maintain control as new settlers moved into the east. Between 1820 and 1830 there were essentially three major geographic regions in Mississippi that voted in blocks on most major issues. These were the seven counties that formed the old Natchez District, the ten counties that constituted the Piney Woods, and the seven new counties created from land acquired through the Treaty of Doak's Stand. The latter were referred to collectively as the New Purchase. While the Tombigbee area in the northeastern portion of the state was also settled, its isolation and lack of population precluded it from having significant impact on government affairs during this period.

The old Natchez District continued to hold the majority of the state's wealth through the decade, but new settlers entering the Piney Woods, and especially the New Purchase area, diluted its political strength. By 1830 a majority of Mississippi's white population lay outside the district's borders, signaling the end of Natchez's political supremacy. Wealth could still buy influence in many quarters, but as a minority in terms of population, leaders of the old Natchez District found it increasingly difficult to control the state legislature or find the votes needed to win statewide elections.

While the Natchez District still wielded formidable power through the 1820s, the eastern counties flexed their political muscles and garnered a number of victories during the period. In one significant instance, western Adams County representation in the Mississippi Legislature was notably reduced. Between 1819 and 1830, with the western counties clearly in control, the legislature removed one senator and two representatives from Adams County

Rosalie

One of grandest mansions of antebellum Natchez, Rosalie was built in 1820–1823 on a high bluff overlooking the Mississippi River, near the sight of the Natchez Indians' massacre of the French at Fort Rosalie a century earlier. It was originally the home of Peter and Eliza Little, whose fortune stemmed from cotton plantations in Louisiana and from one of the first steam-powered lumber mills on the Mississippi. The house was typical of those built by the Natchez elite as they struggled to best one another in displays of opulence and ostentation. After Peter Little's death Andrew Wilson purchased Rosalie, and his descendants occupied the home for several generations. After Natchez surrendered to federal authorities during the Civil War, Rosalie served as the headquarters for the Union army, and Ulysses S. Grant briefly visited the property.

In 1938 the Mississippi State Society of the Daughters of the American Revolution purchased Rosalie and opened it to the public. Today the Federal-style mansion, with its Doric columns, wide galleries, and Colonial fanlights, rests inside an antique cypress fence adjoining a four-acre park that overlooks the Mississippi River. The home is open for tours throughout the year, and the site plays host to the annual Great Mississippi River Balloon Competition and Festival each October.

Photo of Rosalie mansion taken on March 29, 1934 by Ralph Clynne. Courtesy of the Library of Congress.

(which included the city of Natchez). The western counties united to fight this change while the eastern counties unanimously backed the reapportionment, which in effect cut representation for Adams County in half. In another victory, the eastern counties succeeded in electing their candidate, Powhatan Ellis, to a six-year term as United States senator in 1827, and in 1829 they sent an eastern man, Franklin E. Plummer, to the United States House of Representatives. Perhaps the most visible win for the east came in 1821, when eastern representatives forced the relocation of the state capital from Natchez to a more centrally located site. The site chosen was on the Pearl River in the New Purchase. The legislature named the new capital city Jackson, out of reverence to the war hero who had negotiated the Treaty of Doak's Stand. The ultimate triumph of the east over the west came in 1832, when the state adopted a more democratic constitution that would carry it through the remainder of the antebellum period.

THE JACKSONIAN ERA

While sectional alliances were apparent in Mississippi during the 1820s, there were no competing political parties. From statehood to the presidential election year 1832, the Jeffersonian Republicans were the only organized political party in the state. Even the Natchez elites, many of whom resembled the old Federalists in appearance and outlook, carried that moniker. From 1824 to 1832 intra-party factions competed for political supremacy, and in the absence of competing parties, emotionally charged personality politics became the focus. As settlers of a frontier state, most Mississippians were isolated, and the immediacy of local concerns took precedence over national events. As a result, political movements tended to form at the local level around individual leaders, county interests, or a single issue. Legislators won elections largely because of their stances on local issues, coupled with force of personality and oratory skills on the stump.

Grounded in personality politics and intra-state sectionalism that pitted the "haves" of the old Natchez District against the "have nots" of the Piney Woods and New Purchase regions, Mississippi offered fertile political soil for the growth of the national political upheaval of the 1820s

The Old Capitol

Shortly after Mississippi adopted its second constitution in 1832, the state legislature allocated funds for the construction of a new brick capitol building in Jackson to replace an outdated wooden structure. Originally called the State House, the building was first used for official business in 1839. It was built using slave labor and upon its completion was the centerpiece of a state capital that was still little more than a frontier village. As the official seat of Mississippi's government for more than sixty years, the State House played host to many important nineteenth century events. In 1840 programs honoring Andrew Jackson were held at the capitol during the former president's last visit to the city that bore his name. In 1846 volunteers under the command of Jefferson Davis gathered at the State House before leaving for war against Mexico. Fifteen years later the Mississippi Secession convention met at the State House and severed the state's ties with the federal union. During Reconstruction, Hiram Revels, the first African American to serve in the United States Senate, was elected by the legislature during sessions at the capitol.

The State House was replaced in 1903 when a new, more elaborate capitol building was dedicated. The "Old Capitol," as it then came to be known, housed state offices until 1959, when officials initiated a two-year project to restore the building as a museum. Today the Old Capitol Museum remains one of the finest examples of Greek Revival public architecture in the United States. Administered by the Mississippi Department of Archives and History, the building houses the state's historical museum, which includes fascinating exhibits on Mississippi's prehistory, the colonial and territorial periods, the Civil War and Reconstruction, and the civil rights movement.

commonly referred to as Jacksonian Democracy. In Mississippi the movement manifested itself through the direct personal appeal of Andrew Jackson. Jackson's personal popularity in most circles overwhelmed his stand on individual political issues. He was revered in Mississippi as a war hero. The Battle of Horseshoe Bend had been fought in the Mississippi Territory, and his victory over the British at New Orleans—in which many Mississippians took part—captured the hearts and imaginations of the state's residents.

Mississippians also related to Jackson as the product of a frontier society, and they took seriously the so-called "rise of the common man," which he embodied. Finally, Mississippians admired Jackson as a fellow westerner who shared their views concerning Indians. The New Purchase was filled with farmers who credited Jackson personally with removing the Choctaws and allowing the farmers to build homes and start new lives. When compared to their love for the man, most Mississippians had little interest in his position on national issues. To the farmers in the state he was the quintessential American hero.

Though unsuccessful at the national level, Jackson's 1824 presidential campaign in Mississippi was yet another signal that political dominance in the state was shifting from the river counties to the more recently settled areas. At the time the state had only seven newspapers, all of which circulated primarily in the more literate Natchez region. Of these, only one actively backed Jackson, whose chief rival, John Quincy Adams, enjoyed the support of most of the Natchez establishment. The poorer whites in the river counties and those settlers who occupied the Piney Woods and New Purchase regions opposed Adams. Jackson's war record undermined Adams's backers, and most never publicly renounced the old hero. Instead, they emphasized Adams's intellect and statesmanship, qualities that lacked appeal to frontier settlers more concerned with their own survival than with ideological discussions. Jackson lost the national election for the presidency in 1824, but in Mississippi he carried every county.

By 1826 Jacksonianism had completely enveloped Mississippi. That year a staunch Jacksonian, William Haile, won election to the United States House of Representatives and Powahatan Ellis defeated Thomas B. Reed in a contest for the United States Senate. Reed's primary weakness during the campaign was the perception that he was not completely in support of Jackson. As the presidential contest approached, many Mississippi politicians who had been lukewarm about Jackson's candidacy, and some who had previously opposed him, scrambled to jump on the Jacksonian bandwagon. In November of 1828, Jackson was elected president, again winning every county in Mississippi and outpolling Adams 6,714 to 1,674. The same

George Poindexter

No Mississippi politician was more influential during the territorial and early statehood periods than George Poindexter. Born in Virginia in 1779, Poindexter moved to Natchez at the age of twenty-three, started a law practice, and two years later began his rapid rise in politics with an appointment as attorney general of the Mississippi Territory. Poindexter represented the territory in Washington as a territorial delegate from 1807 to 1813 and practically wrote Mississippi's first constitution. He was Mississippi's first representative to Congress (1817–1819) and the state's second governor (1820–1822). In 1830 the state legislature elected Poindexter to the United States Senate.

After going to Washington as a senator, Poindexter's political fortunes began to fade. Poindexter clashed with President Andrew Jackson on a number of issues, to the point that their political disputes became personal. The two ill-tempered men despised one another, which doomed Poindexter's future in the nation's capital. In 1836 he lost his bid for reelection to a candidate who had popular Jackson's unqualified endorsement. Poindexter continued practicing law, but his feud with Jackson made it impossible for him to regain his political footing. He suffered a series of personal tragedies and moved out of the state for a time. An embittered Poindexter later returned to Jackson, Mississippi, where he practiced law in the city named for his chief political enemy. He died in Jackson in 1855 and was buried in Greenwood Cemetery.

support was shown four years later during his successful bid for reelection. To the common citizen he remained a hero, and to the practical politician the Jacksonian movement proved irresistible. During some campaigns, candidates abandoned the issues completely and instead focused on "out-Jacksoning" one another.

Despite his overwhelming popularity, Andrew Jackson was not without enemies in Mississippi. Many of the wealthy Natchez elite came to despise the president. While they may have admired his war record, it was difficult for them to support such a rough politician over more well-educated, dignified statesmen. The Natchez elite also bristled at the prospect of ordinary citizens, such as the small farmers of the Piney Woods and New Purchase, taking an active role in state government. To many conservative Natchez politicians, Jackson was a symbol of everything they feared in terms of political reform and popular participation in the political process. As a result, many of the state's wealthier elements would form the nucleus of the Mississippi Whig Party during Jackson's second term.

During Jackson's administration, the federal government completed the process of Indian removal in the Mississippi. In 1830 Jackson sent Secretary of War John Eaton to the state to negotiate with the Choctaws for the remainder of their lands. As with the Doak's Stand negotiations ten years earlier, the discussions led to threats and intimidation. The Choctaws eventually accepted the Treaty of Dancing Rabbit Creek, named for a stream near the meeting site, and most began the actual removal process. The Chickasaws succumbed two years later. Final removal of the Indians predictably set in motion another great flood of settlers into the state and led to the creation of almost thirty new counties. As a result, the population of Mississippi increased dramatically—almost threefold— from 1830 to 1840. As with the settlement of the New Purchase, immigrants to these new counties were primarily small farmers, many of whom credited Andrew Jackson personally for removing the Indians. Their arrival drove the final nail in the coffin of Natchez dominance in Mississippi politics.

Mississippi's Second Constitution

By the early 1830s Mississippi's original constitution was obsolete. It lacked any procedures for amendment and provided an ill-fitting governmental framework for a state experiencing steady growth. Through the 1820s, calls for a new constitutional convention had met with little success due to sectionalism. The Piney Woods and New Purchase sections backed periodic proposals for a convention in hopes that it would produce a document that would address their concerns, while the Natchez District blocked such efforts for fear that a new constitution would undermine their dominance in the state. As the Indian removal process

Population Statistics

Census Year	Free White	Slave
1820	42,175	33,272
1830	70,433	65,659
1840	179,074	195,211

progressed, however, the river counties' political leadership withdrew their opposition, believing that it would be in their best interest to hold a constitutional convention before more new counties could be organized. At a general election held in August of 1831 Mississippi voters overwhelmingly approved the convention. The following year voters selected convention delegates who met in Jackson between September 10 and October 26, 1832.

The Mississippi Constitution of 1832 codified a number of the central tenets of Jacksonian Democracy, such as the removal of property requirements for franchise and office holding, and the popular election of almost all state and local officials. Most of these reforms encountered little opposition and were generally taken for granted by the delegates, even those from the river counties. While some sectional animosity was evident, and there were spirited exchanges concerning certain issues, the convention adopted the new constitution over relatively little dissent. For adult white males the end result was the most democratic constitution in the South and one of the most democratic in the nation at the time. In addition to extending the franchise, the new constitution included a liberal amendment procedure, abolished life tenure for office holders, and made Mississippi the only state in the nation that elected all of its judges. Ironically, while it likely would have passed by a large margin, the most democratic constitution in the South was not submitted to the people for ratification.

RELIGION

During (and after) the antebellum period, the actively religious among the Deep South's population were almost exclusively Protestant. Evangelicals populated most of the region, with Baptists, Methodists, and Presbyterians representing the major denominations. Baptist and Methodist congregations were by far the most numerous. By comparison, the Presbyterian requirements for an educated clergy and a theology more intellectual than emotional in character somewhat hampered their growth. At the turn of the nineteenth century, around 10 percent of whites in the South belonged to a church, but within a short time a great spiritual awakening took hold through much of the region. Sparked by revivals in south-central Kentucky during the summer of 1800, evangelical religion swept though the southern states and thousands of converts swelled church memberships. By 1860 at least 40 percent of white Southerners actively participated in organized churches. Even in areas where a majority of the population did not regularly attend meetings, churches exerted influence. They were the social centers of many communities, places where locals gathered both to worship and to take part in secular fellowship. Ministers, usually recognized as the definitive moral arbiters in individual communities, often held sway over public opinion on a variety of issues not necessarily religious in nature.

Baptists, Methodists, and Presbyterians had all penetrated the Mississippi Territory by the turn of the nineteenth century, and each denomination would grow over the next several decades. Of Mississippi's 1,441 churches on the eve of the Civil War, 83 percent were either Baptist or Methodist, while 10 percent, still exerting significant influence despite their relatively small number, were Presbyterian. The remaining seven percent included scattered congregations of Episcopalians, Lutherans, Disciples of Christ, and Catholics.

EDUCATION

During the antebellum period Mississippi had no organized public school system. Planters usually hired private tutors, or had their children educated in the North or abroad. While the state periodically levied special school taxes or appropriated special funds, many children in rural areas had no access to education. Even communities that had the private resources for schools usually only provided for the elementary grades. Most of Mississippi's first schools were housed in small log structures with primitive furnishings where students sat on rough plank benches to hear their lessons. Public higher education finally came to the state in 1848 when the University of Mississippi opened its doors at Oxford with four faculty members and eighty students. Funding for the new university was pledged by the state legislature from the sale of federal lands.

While public education made little progress in antebellum Mississippi, a number of private schools began operation during the territorial and early statehood periods. The state's first educational institution, Jefferson College, was chartered by the territorial legislature in 1802. Located in Washington, just outside of Natchez, the school depended primarily on an irregular flow of private funds. As a result, it did not open its doors to students until 1811, nine years after it received its charter. In 1818, in Washington, the Methodists established Elizabeth Female Academy, one of the first institutions in the United States to confer degrees on women, and three years later Franklin Academy opened in Columbus with the help of federal funds. Over the next few years Hampstead Academy was organized in Clinton and the Presbyterians organized Oakland College in Rodney. Hampstead Academy later became Mississippi College, a Baptist school and the state's oldest institution of higher learning still in operation.

THE SPREAD OF SLAVERY AND CHANGING ATTITUDES

By 1840 Mississippi was the nation's leading cotton producer. While most of the state's cotton still came from the old Natchez District, the New Purchase region contributed significantly to the state's total. Many of the western counties of the Choctaw and Chickasaw Cessions developed their own plantation economy just as rapidly. As the cotton market in Mississippi expanded, so did the institution of slavery. High concentrations of slaves were no longer confined to counties in the old Natchez District. Whites were in the minority in most of the counties in the western half of the state. In contrast, most eastern counties, the domain of the non-slaveholding subsistence farmer, produced relatively little cotton and were white in majority.

Jefferson College

The Mississippi Territorial legislature chartered Mississippi's first educational institution on May 13, 1802. Named for the nation's third president, Jefferson College opened its doors to students in 1811, and among its alumni were some of the state's early leaders, including Jefferson Davis. For years prior to the Civil War the school was a major influence on the intellectual and cultural development of the Mississippi frontier. Not only did some of the state's leading citizens send their sons to Jefferson College, but the school's administrative officers, faculty, and students participated in early agricultural and scientific experiments that helped direct the course of Mississippi's development in the first half of the nineteenth century.

During the Civil War Jefferson College closed, only to reopen again in 1866 as a preparatory school. While it remained in operation for another century, the school would never reclaim its place as a center of the state's intellectual community. By the turn of the twentieth century the school was known as Jefferson Military College, and it retained that name until 1964, when the school closed its doors for the last time. Today the building and grounds of Historic Jefferson College are administered by the Mississippi Department of Archives and History and are open to the public. Visitors can tour the restored buildings that include exhibits related to the school's past. Historic Jefferson College is located six miles east of Natchez in Washington, Mississippi, on land that it has occupied for almost two centuries.

Jefferson College photo by James Butters, April 15, 1936.
Image courtesy of the Library of Congress.

Top Cotton Producing States, 1840

Mississippi
Georgia
Louisiana
Alabama
South Carolina

In the east only a small area confined to the fertile, long-settled Tombigbee region held a majority slave population.

The increase in cotton production changed opinions in Mississippi with regard to the institution of slavery. While slavery had been present in Mississippi virtually from the time the first Europeans appeared, Mississippians of the territorial and early statehood periods were uncomfortable with the institution. Many public officials even talked of ending slavery in the state, but no one could come up with what they considered a reasonable plan to do so. As late as 1831 many state leaders still viewed slavery as a "necessary evil." However, this sentiment would soon fade. During the 1830s the opening of the new Indian lands and rising cotton prices brought more slaves into Mississippi, and by 1840 slaves represented more than half of the state's total population. Suddenly, ending slavery was no longer discussed. Instead, Mississippians began justifying and even praising slavery as a positive institution. Even many members of the Mississippi clergy actively promoted slavery, claiming that it was sanctioned by the Bible.

Like the rest of the South, Mississippi's defense of the institution of slavery intensified as the abolition movement grew in the North. The perceived threat to slavery united most white residents of the region, rich and poor, large slaveholders, small slaveholders, and non-slaveholders alike. Though many whites likely recognized the injustice of slavery, racism left most in a dilemma that would not reconcile itself. Although literally surrounded by blacks, they could not conceive of a free, biracial society. Slavery defined the self-perception of every white Mississippian and every white Southerner. For the planter elite, holding slaves signified power and status, and a disruption of the slave system meant the potential disruption of the planter's larger societal authority. The planters enjoyed their elite position in the slaveholding world, and they were determined to defend and maintain it.

The impact was similar on poorer, non-slaveholding white males. Though not directly involved as slaveholders, they recognized the social impact that the demise of slavery would have on their world. Regardless of their economic condition, they drew strength and self-esteem simply from the fact that they were white males and heads of their own households. Their white skin bonded them to their more affluent planter neighbors, with whom they periodically interacted. They recognized the importance of property as the traditional barometer of independence and feared a future in which they might compete with free blacks for land or in the labor market. Many small farmers also aspired to become prominent, slave-holding planters one day. The South's slave-based society allowed poorer white males the comfort of viewing themselves as free men in a society where most of the population was not free. They defined their own independence through the bondage of others, and believed that the demise of slavery represented a negative impact on their status in the community.

4

THE CRISIS YEARS, 1846–1861

By the late 1840s danger loomed just over the horizon for Mississippi and for the rest of the nation. The United States' acquisition of vast amounts of western territory as a result of the Mexican War opened the slavery debate in earnest and lit the fuse that would ignite the Civil War. Mississippi, one of the major slaveholding states, was heavily involved in the slavery controversy. As in the rest of the Deep South, by the 1850s a distinct "way of life" based on preservation of slavery had developed in the state. This way of life would lead Mississippi to break from the Union after less than half a century as a state.

THE MEXICAN WAR

In 1846, years of tension between the United States and Mexico erupted into war over a border dispute in southern Texas. Southern congressmen, who coveted Mexican possessions in the west, promoted the war in hopes of spreading slavery into any conquered territories. As the war got underway many Mississippians, along with other Southerners, responded to the call to arms. Part of this response was due to a deep-seated belief that military service was an essential part of their heritage. Tales of the bravery of Southerners during the American Revolution, the War of 1812, and in various conflicts against Indians were tightly woven into the fabric of the southern existence. Such stories, either factual or embellished, transformed common men into heroes, and the concepts of honor and self-worth for many Southerners were derived from the fact that their family lineage included soldiers who would, without hesitation, "leap at the first blast of the trumpet." Patriotism ran high during the Mexican war as communities all over Mississippi collected funds and contributed troops to the war effort. There was little doubt in the minds of most that the war would end in a great American victory, winning praise and glory for all those who participated.

Despite the fact that the United States was fighting with questionable motives against an overmatched foe, and the reality that more soldiers died from disease than battle wounds during the conflict, the Mexican War was a triumph for the South and for Mississippi. The hostilities produced nationally acclaimed Mississippi war heroes, including Jefferson Davis and John A. Quitman, but more importantly it produced community heroes as well. Veterans returned home with firmly established reputations as honorable men. Those who lost their lives during the struggle, whether from wounds or disease, were honored as community martyrs. In this way, community participation had localized the war, given individual communities a stake in its outcome, and caused the war's end to be celebrated as a community victory. In addition to bolstering community pride, the Mexican War had more far-reaching influences on Mississippi. Just as community participation localized the military effort, it also localized subsequent national issues that were products of the war's outcome. Paramount among these was the issue of slavery and its spread into the newly acquired western territories.

WILMOT PROVISO

Even before the war with Mexico was over, controversy began in the United States Congress as a representative from Pennsylvania named David Wilmot introduced an amendment to an appropriations bill that became known as the Wilmot Proviso. The Wilmot Proviso prohibited slavery in any territory acquired from Mexico as a result of the war. The bill to which Wilmot's amendment was attached passed the House of Representatives but failed in the Senate. Despite this, the Wilmot Proviso's mere introduction fueled the slavery debate. Southern militants were enraged, and over the next few years they would make repeated reference to the legislation in their rhetoric. They made speeches and wrote newspapers editorials warning that the South should be on guard and used the Wilmot Proviso to allege that there was an abolitionist conspiracy underway in the North, a conspiracy designed to take away the property of white

John A. Quitman

The son of a Lutheran minister, John Anthony Quitman was born in Rhinebeck, New York in 1799. He studied law and in his early twenties moved to Natchez, where he was determined to make a name for himself. He established a law practice and rapidly ascended the Natchez social ladder. Within a decade his law practice and successful land speculation had made Quitman a member of the prominent planter class in the city. He entered politics, securing a place in the state legislature in 1827. The following year he was elected chancellor of the state, a position he held until entering the state senate several years later. Quitman was elected president of the senate and in 1835–1836 he served as acting governor of Mississippi. Quitman made a national name for himself during the Mexican War as a brigadier general commanding volunteers at the Battle of Monteray. His command was the first to enter Mexico City after its surrender and Quitman served briefly as civil and military governor of the city. He returned to Mississippi where he was elected governor in 1849. For the rest of his career Quitman was Mississippi's leading proponent of states' rights, and his speeches were quoted throughout the South as the Civil War approached. He was elected to the United States Congress in 1854 and reelected two years later. Though an advocate of secession as a potential remedy to national problems, Quitman did not live to see the dissolution of the Union. He died on July 17, 1858 at his plantation in Natchez.

Southerners, deny white Southerners their rights under the Constitution, and end the so-called "Southern way of life." Southern militants had their own ideas about what should happen to any territory acquired from Mexico. They claimed that the territories belonged to the entire nation, and that all Americans had a right to them, including the right to move their slaves into the new territory. They considered slaves property, and argued that a slaveholder had the right to maintain his property anywhere that the United States had jurisdiction. In short, they took the position that slavery could not be banned in the United States by anyone, under any circumstance.

For residents of Mississippi, proposals to halt slavery's expansion in the years following the war were not merely

David Wilmot engraving by Morris H. Traubel, created between 1887 and 1900. Provided by the Libary of Congress.

the distant maneuverings of northern politicians at the national level. They represented an effort to deny the South the spoils of war that hometown heroes had helped win and, as such, were an affront to the individual community's support for the war effort. These were insults that could not, and would not, be easily forgotten. As sectional tensions increased, self-serving local politicians, as well as those at the state and national level, used racial politics as they reminded their constituents again and again that all white Mississippians, and indeed all white southerners, were under attack by those who would deny the slaveholding South its rights.

SLAVERY AND THE 1850S

Through the late 1840s and 1850s, Mississippi's population increased dramatically, from 375,651 in 1840 to 791,305 in 1860. During this period many communities had become well established, with networks of dirt roads linking towns to one another and to the state's developing markets. As communication and transportation improved, Mississippians were increasingly affected by events taking place outside their immediate vicinity. Most communities had access to a local newspaper that, in addition to reporting local events, kept readers apprised of state and national politics, usually with a partisan slant. The outside world was encroaching on even the most isolated settlements,

Holly Springs

Settled since the 1820s, Holly Springs became Marshall County's seat of government with the establishment of the county in 1836. From the Mexican War until the Civil War, Holly Springs was a boom town and a major hub of northern Mississippi's cotton economy. In 1850 Marshall County's population was larger than that of any other county in the state, and Holly Springs and the surrounding area produced more than 30,000 bales of cotton annually. Mansions sprung up in Holly Springs seemingly overnight, and the town's streets bustled with activity. Antebellum Marshall County was known as the "Empire County" as a result of its great prosperity. During the Civil War, Holly Springs survived dozens of raids and, for a time, served as General Grant's headquarters in northern Mississippi. The town survived another great test in 1878 when the yellow fever epidemic carried away many of its citizens.

Today Holly Springs is still Marshall County's seat of government. The city boasts more than 7,000 residents as well as 64 antebellum structures, including churches, modest homes, and a number of huge mansions. The annual Holly Springs Pilgrimage is Mississippi's second oldest (after the Natchez Pilgrimage) and attracts thousands of visitors every year. In a testament to the area's cultural diversity, the town's Hill Crest Cemetery is the final resting place of several Confederate generals as well as Hiram Revels, the first African American to serve in the United States Senate. Anti-lynching advocate Ida B. Wells was born in Holly Springs, and the town also includes Rust College, Mississippi's oldest historically black college. The impressive Marshall County Museum, located just off the town square in Holly Springs, includes three floors and twenty-two rooms containing more than 40,000 items relating to the area's history.

making it difficult for anyone in Mississippi to ignore the most singularly significant issue of the day.

By the 1850s Mississippi was deeply entrenched in the socioeconomic quagmire of slavery. From the time the state entered the Union through the end of the antebellum period, its economic, political, and social foundations rested squarely on agriculture and increasingly on a slavery-based cotton culture. During the 1850s Mississippi continued to establish itself as the one of the nation's top cotton producers. In 1859, the state produced a record 1,202,507 ginned bales of cotton, leading production in the southern states and constituting more than one-fifth of the United States' total. For the well-to-do planters of the era, the 1850s were a time of great prosperity, evidenced by the fact that during that ten-year period the value of farm lands in Mississippi increased by 176%. Of course, Mississippi's cotton kingdom was built by slave labor, and by 1860 slaves represented 55% of the state's total population.

From the end of the Mexican War the slavery issue drove Mississippi politics. It helped destroy the state's Whig Party, whose national apparatus had become too closely associated with northern abolitionism to suit most Southerners. Ultimately, the issue of slavery allowed the state's right wing of the Democratic Party to emerge unchallenged. A fledgling states' rights movement had developed in Mississippi as early as the 1830s, but its leaders were unable to influence significant numbers of voters. Following the Mexican War, however, states' rights advocates pointed to the Wilmot Proviso and speeches by northern politicians as tangible evidence that an abolitionist conspiracy existed in the North. They exploited fear to

Mississippi Population Statistics, 1840–1860

Year	Free White	Slave
1840	179,074	195,211
1850	295,718	309,874
1860	353,899	436,631

draw voters to their cause, using exhaustive rhetoric that centered around the demise of slavery and the subsequent breakdown of southern communities and white culture once emancipation had taken place.

This argument was increasingly potent in a state where the white population was in the minority. After extensive and prolonged debate, the Mississippi Legislature voted to accept the Compromise of 1850, and in 1851 the state narrowly elected a governor who had run on a pro-Union platform. After the Kansas agitation of 1854, however, states' rights politicians had enough rhetorical ammunition to make the abolitionist threat real in the minds of many Mississippians. For the rest of the decade Mississippi Democrats consolidated their strength around a strict states' rights platform, which had at its foundation the protection of slavery at all costs. This position left no room for compromise, and at the end of the 1850s it lit the fuse that would ignite civil war.

After 1855 Democratic candidates carried most Mississippi counties in state and national elections. All of the factions vying for leadership positions within the state's Democratic Party knew that they could not achieve their goals without embracing the states' rights philosophy. Political leaders at the county level used states' rights rhetoric in speeches that, while not necessarily inciting their constituents to radical action, made sectional tensions a part of local discourse. Across Mississippi citizens held meetings to discuss current political issues, all of which had become tied in one way or another to the slavery debate. While most of these meetings did not directly advocate secession as a singular course of action, they did cross an important threshold because most recognized secession as a possible solution to sectional tensions. They also brought the slavery question into individual counties and planted it firmly at the doorstep of anyone who took part in day-to-day community conversations.

The message was clear. A threat to slavery was not simply a threat to the property of slaveholders. The demise of the institution would also lead to chaos and violence that would expose all whites to danger. Democratic leaders throughout Mississippi took advantage of these fears (which their party had helped to create) by constantly

Henry Stuart Foote

Henry Stuart Foote's long-winded bravado and general irascibility made him one of the most controversial political figures in the United States during the middle decades of the nineteenth century. Born in Fauquier County, Virginia on February 28, 1804, he moved to Mississippi as a young man, settling first in Vicksburg and then in Jackson, where he built up one of the state's most lucrative law practices. He was a vocal supporter of Andrew Jackson and quickly established himself as an influential member of Mississippi's political community. During the 1840s Foote represented Mississippi in the United States Senate, where his abrasive personality made him unpopular among other senators. Foote and fellow senator Jefferson Davis particularly despised one another, and the hard feelings between them surfaced on Christmas Day, 1847, when they actually came to blows in the parlor of a Washington, DC rooming house during a political discussion.

In 1851, following heated debates in Congress over the Compromise of 1850, Foote and Davis ran against one another for governor of Mississippi. Sensing that most Mississippians were, at the time, tiring of sectional bickering, Foote based his campaign on Mississippi's loyalty to the Union and defeated Davis by a slim margin. He served as governor until 1854. Still urging support for the Union, Foote relocated to Nashville. He eventually backed secession once it became inevitable and won a seat in the Confederate Congress representing Tennessee's Fifth Congressional District. As a Confederate lawmaker, he continued to be a thorn in Davis's side by relentlessly questioning the president's leadership. After the war Foote wrote several books and articles on antebellum politics, many of which were highly critical of Davis. Henry Foote died in 1880 and was buried in Nashville.

reminding the masses that the Democratic Party was the party of the South, and the party dedicated to the protection of slavery at all costs. By inciting fear among their constituents, states' rights Democrats ran roughshod over what little political competition existed at both the local and state levels. They continued their rhetorical onslaught through the 1850s until most voices of reason in their party had been either converted or silenced.

According to one local politician of the period, many citizens eventually accepted states' rights rhetoric as fact simply because "it had been so often sounded in their ears that they had become somewhat accustomed to it." In 1859 John Jones Pettus, a stalwart states' rights Democrat, won the governorship with a landslide 77 percent of the vote.

Jacinto Courthouse

During the mid-nineteenth century the town of Jacinto was flourishing in northeastern Mississippi. Shops, taverns, a newspaper, and several churches lined its streets, and the town boasted a boys' school that attracted students from three states. As the county seat of Tishomingo County (now Alcorn County), Jacinto was an important political center, and the imposing Jacinto Court House was the center of town life. Completed in 1854, the two-story building was constructed with handmade bricks and has been called one of the best examples of federal style architecture in the South.

Unfortunately, as the courthouse was being built the town of Jacinto was living on borrowed time. Bypassed by the railroad and not chosen as a seat of government when county lines in the region were redrawn during Reconstruction, Jacinto's population began to decline. The courthouse was used as a school until 1908 and then as a Methodist Church until 1960. In 1964 volunteers rescued the structure from scheduled demolition, and through their efforts the building was restored and placed on the National Register of Historic Places. Today Jacinto is a ghost town, but the courthouse is open to the public. The Jacinto Foundation administers the building as a museum and also operates a nearby "country store" containing a variety of souvenirs and handmade gifts.

JOHN BROWN AND HARPER'S FERRY

On October 16, 1859 the fanatic abolitionist John Brown and a small group of followers captured the federal arsenal at Harper's Ferry, Virginia. Brown planned to use the weapons there to arm area slaves, inciting them into open rebellion, and creating a formidable army to wreak havoc in the Virginia countryside. Brown's scheme was ill conceived from the outset. After he and his followers captured the arsenal, local townspeople held the group at bay until federal troops could be summoned.

Federal troops captured Brown and he was hanged for treason. However, word of his plot struck fear into the hearts of white Southerners and played into the hands of radical southern politicians, especially after many Northerners praised Brown as a hero (Ralph Waldo Emerson compared Brown to Jesus Christ). In Mississippi, newly-elected governor John J. Pettus told his constituents that they should prepare to do battle because "[t]he scene at Harper's Ferry is not the end, but in my opinion only the beginning of the end of the conflict." The state's Democratic press kept rumors of slave revolts alive and circulating after the Brown incident, and in Jackson the legislature appropriated $150,000 to reorganize and arm the state's volunteer militia in preparation for further conflict. Other southern states followed suit, reorganizing their forces in what turned out to be a precursor to the organization of the Confederate army.

THE 1860 PRESIDENTIAL ELECTION

During the spring of 1860 the slavery issue split the national Democratic Party, thus insuring a Republican victory in the presidential election the following fall. The Democratic National Convention met in April at Charleston, South Carolina, where northern Democrats passed resolutions endorsing the concept of popular sovereignty as a solution to the slavery problem. Meanwhile, southern Democrats insisted on federal protection of the institution. The convention endorsed popular sovereignty, and in response delegates from Mississippi and other southern states walked out of the proceedings. Eventually, the two factions of the party met separately to nominate candidates for president. Northern Democrats nominated Stephen Douglas of Illinois, while the southern states' rights advocates chose the vice-president of the United States, Kentuckian John C. Breckinridge, as their candidate. John Bell of Tennessee rounded out the field that would oppose Republican Abraham Lincoln. Bell was the candidate of the recently formed Constitutional Union Party, whose members hoped to create an alternative organization based on an allegiance to the Constitution and the Union that would appeal to both sections. They accused southern Democratic leaders of abandoning the protection of southern liberties in favor of personal political gain through the secession movement. They further argued that Southerners should fight for their rights within the Union, and did their best to sidestep any inflammatory political discussions about slavery. The strategy had only limited effect in the southern states, where the protection of slavery had become by far the most important political issue.

In November, Lincoln, who was not on Mississippi's ballots and whose countenance one Mississippi Democratic editor described as being "strongly marked with the blood of his Negro ancestry," was elected president of the United States. Quickly, sectional sentiment polarized and ripped the United States apart. The expansion of slavery into the western territories had been the primary issue of the campaign and the victory of Lincoln's "Black Republican" Party seemed to place the South on the verge of realizing its greatest fear: the Republicans insisted on halting the western expansion of slavery, and it was only a matter of time until they pressed for complete abolition. Southern Democratic leaders, whose unyielding stand on the slavery issue had split their national party, began taking steps to use the Republican victory to justify southern secession. These men emphasized their own interpretation of the Constitution. The United States, they claimed, was a collection of sovereign, independent states. Under this theory each state had entered the Union voluntarily, and therefore was free to leave the Union if its citizens felt politically, socially, or morally abused.

Even before Lincoln's inauguration, fissures in the Union had widened. South Carolina voted in convention to secede on December 20, 1860. On January 6, 1861 Florida troops seized the Federal arsenal at Apalachicola, and the next day the state seized Federal Forts Marion and St. Augustine. Within a few weeks several other southern states, including Mississippi, followed South Carolina out of the Union. After the surrender of Fort Sumter on April 13, Lincoln put out the call for 75,000 northern volunteer troops and suddenly the United States was at war with itself.

The Secession Convention

In Mississippi, events moved quickly following Lincoln's election. A number of state political leaders encouraged Governor John Jones Pettus, a firm believer in the right to secede, to act. In the state capital the *Jackson Mississippian* reflected the dominant mood in an editorial entitled, "The Deed is Done, Disunion the Remedy," which was published soon after Lincoln's victory. After consulting Mississippi's congressional delegation, Pettus advised the state legislature that withdrawal from the Union was the only alternative to "Black Republican rule." Believing that such a withdrawal from the Union would be only temporary, and filled with a certain degree of misguided missionary zeal, Pettus told the assembly that it was time for Mississippi to "go down into Egypt while Herod rules in Judea." The legislature responded by passing resolutions sanctioning secession and by calling for a state convention to consider Mississippi's withdrawal from the Union.

In December of 1860 Mississippians elected delegates to the state secession convention on a county-by-county basis. In most counties, elections involved candidates who favored separate state secession and candidates leaning toward southern cooperation. Cooperationists generally took the stand that Lincoln's election alone was not a reason to disrupt the Union. Only after all options within the Union had been exhausted, they argued, should Mississippi consider secession, and then only in concert with the other southern states. Despite this more moderate platform, however, only a few candidates who were labeled cooperationists were firmly against secession.

The convention candidates were not necessarily nominated on a particular platform, even though their public positions on the secession question were well known to their neighbors. A number of factors contributed to the election of pro-secession delegates to the convention. During the canvas the radicals held a distinct advantage. Most of the state's prominent political voices backed secession, and the radical organization that had helped John C. Breckinridge carry the state by a wide margin in the presidential contest remained in place. Each county elected men who were established in local political circles, which meant that most were established within the state Democratic Party network. As such, these men were schooled in the states' rights philosophy of the 1850s and had won their political status with the help of states' rights rhetoric. It was also significant that voter turnout was much lower for the election of convention delegates than for the previous presidential election. Approximately 68,000 voters statewide took part in the presidential contest, while only about 38,000 cast ballots for convention delegates. The lighter turnout favored the secessionists and may have signified a concession by more cautious moderates that the issue of secession had already been decided by Lincoln's election. In general, many voters were willing to support more radical action when faced with a Republican poised to occupy the White House. After Lincoln's election much of the public was more agitated with regard to the slavery issue, and secessionists became more likely to use various forms of intimidation to accomplish their goals. Such was the case with one voter who later claimed that he cast his ballot for an anti-secession candidate "amidst the frowns, murmurs, and threats of the judges and bystanders" at the polls.

The Mississippi Secession Convention met in Jackson on January 7, 1861. Although some cooperationist delegates voiced opposition to the state exiting the union, conciliatory rhetoric quickly faded in the face of a decidedly pro-secession majority. Three amendments to fend off immediate secession did come before the convention, including one proposing that a secession ordinance should not go into effect until ratified by the state's voters in a popular referendum, but this and the others were handily defeated. Finally, on January 9, an ordinance of secession passed by a vote of 84 to 15. Afterwards, one observer heard a number of confident convention delegates claim that secession would do little more than bring the North to the bargaining table, and that the Union would be restored in less than a year. Only two delegates, John W. Wood of Attala County and John J. Thornton of Rankin County, failed to sign the ordinance after it was passed.

The convention published both the ordinance and *A Declaration of the Immediate Causes of Secession*. The declaration left little doubt concerning the primary reason for Mississippi leaving the Union:

Mississippi Governor's Mansion

Completed in 1842 at a cost of just over $60,000, the Mississippi Governor's Mansion in Jackson is the second oldest continually occupied governor's residence in the United States. State architect William Nichols incorporated classic Greek Revival architecture in the mansion's design in an attempt to "adhere to a plain republican simplicity." Through the years the mansion played host to many notable American personalities when they visited the capital city. It survived the Civil War but was threatened soon after the turn of the twentieth century when the state legislature considered razing the downtown structure in favor of commercial development. The plan collapsed amid public outrage that asked "Will Mississippi destroy what Sherman did not burn?" Plans to demolish the building were replaced with plans for a major renovation, completed in 1909. During the 1940s the mansion was further restored, and thirty years later a $2.7 million renovation project produced the historic showplace that visitors can tour today in downtown Jackson.

Governor's Mansion, 316 East Capitol Street, Jackson. Photos by Jack E. Boucher, 1936. Courtesy of the Library of Congress.

Our position is thoroughly identified with slavery—the greatest material institution in the world. Its labor supplies the products, which constitute by far the largest and most important portions of the commerce of the earth. These products are peculiar to the climate verging on the tropical regions, and by an imperious law of nature, none but the black race can bear exposure to the tropical sun. These products have become necessities to the world, and a blow at slavery is a blow at commerce and civilization…. There was no choice left to us but submission to the mandates of abolition, or a dissolution of the Union, whose principles had been subverted to work out our ruin.

After severing Mississippi's ties with the United States, the secession convention remained in session for the purpose of revising the government of what some referred to as the Republic of Mississippi. Among other business, the convention modified the existing state constitution, appointed a major general and four brigadiers, adopted an official flag, and elected delegates to a convention to meet in Montgomery, Alabama for the purpose of creating a southern confederacy. The convention adjourned on January 26 and reconvened two months later to ratify the constitution of the Confederate States of America.

While the Mississippi Secession Convention officially took the state out of the Union, the fight for southern independence had not yet begun. A violent struggle of unmatched proportion was close at hand as decades of alarmist rhetoric evolved into action. Rather than a second American Revolution, as many Southerners claimed, secession proved to be a fatal fit of temper. Citizens throughout Mississippi would soon feel the full impact of their state's decision to leave the Union.

5

The Civil War, 1861–1865

Once secession became a reality in Mississippi, young men were not timid in turning out to defend their native state and newly established nation. Enthusiasm ran high as thousands volunteered to take part in what most believed would be a relatively easy struggle. In the South, the prevailing viewpoint was that one Southerner equaled at least a half dozen Northerners in character, conscience, and convictions. It was absurd—even blasphemous—to believe that a man from the North could best a man from the South at anything. Many Southerners also labored under the mistaken impression that the Northerners did not want to fight, could not fight, and would not fight if forced into a major confrontation. Most ignored the fact that the Southern resources needed to carry out a war effort were sadly lacking when compared to those of the North.

Young men throughout Mississippi volunteered for service to the Confederacy for a number of reasons. Some held a deep-seated hatred for the Yankees that had accumulated from their earliest memories. "Unreasonable" and "oppressive" were adjectives that many had heard since childhood applied to Northern politics and policies. Secessionist politicians had successfully disguised the slavery question as a states' rights issue, underscored by easily exploitable national events. Historically, Northern leaders had challenged the admission of Missouri into the Union as a slave state, advanced the Wilmot Proviso in Congress, supported a variety of national tariffs that the South strongly opposed, and given safe harbor to abolitionists like William Lloyd Garrison and John Brown. The North, it seemed, was determined to deprive Southern citizens of their property, and in so doing, of their independence and constitutionally guaranteed right to the

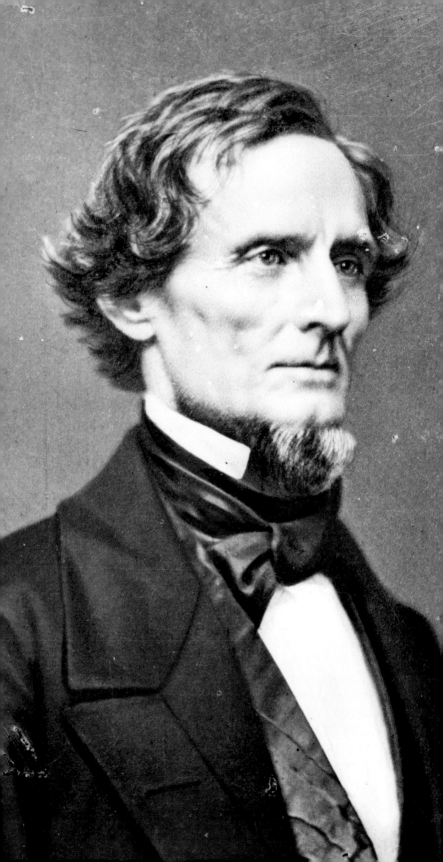

Jefferson Davis

The only president of the Confederacy was born in 1808 in Fairview, Kentucky and, as a young boy, moved with his family to Wilkinson County, Mississippi. At the age of sixteen he received an appointment to the United States Military Academy. He graduated in 1828 and for the next seven years served in the United States Army, where he took part in the Black Hawk War under the command of Zachary Taylor. He eventually married Taylor's daughter, but she died of malaria less than three months after their wedding. Davis resigned his commission and moved back to Mississippi, where in 1845 he won election to the United States Congress and married Varina Howell. With the outbreak of the Mexican War, Davis again joined the army, leading a regiment of Mississippi troops at the Battle of Buena Vista. He was wounded during the fighting and returned home a war hero. In 1850 Mississippi Governor Albert Gallatin Brown appointed Davis to the United States Senate, where he served for three years until he was chosen to be Secretary of War by President Franklin Pierce. Davis later returned to the Senate. While he believed in the right of a state to secede from the Union, he argued against secession in 1861 in hopes of avoiding bloodshed. When Mississippi left the Union, however, he went with it and became president of the Confederacy.

Davis's term as Confederate president was fraught with controversy. At times he clashed with Confederate generals and made questionable decisions that evoked criticism as Confederate casualties mounted. As the Confederate government crumbled in 1865 he attempted to escape, but was captured near Irwinville, Georgia. He was imprisoned until 1868. Davis later retired to Beauvoir, a mansion on the Mississippi Gulf Coast, where he wrote his own history of the Confederacy, *The Rise and Fall of the Confederate Government*. Davis died in 1889.

pursuit of happiness. As a result, many young Confederates, caught up in the patriotic spirit of the day, left home in 1861 as self-proclaimed defenders of not only their state, but of fundamental principles that represented everything they held sacred. In the words of one new recruit, "inflammatory speeches and stirring martial music was the order of the day."

Others were less philosophical. A significant number volunteered for service simply because they feared being ostracized in their communities if they did not. This was particularly true after the draft went into effect in 1862–1863 and a stigma tainted drafted soldiers labeled as "conscripts." A sheer desire for adventure motivated some to enlist. To these men the Confederate Army offered the allure of travel to far-flung destinations, abstract visions of glory, and a unique opportunity to escape the daily drudgery of everyday life. Regardless of their motives, the vast majority of Confederate soldiers during the first year of the war firmly believed in the righteousness of their cause. Even those who had doubts or sensed catastrophe on the horizon rarely expressed their concerns publicly.

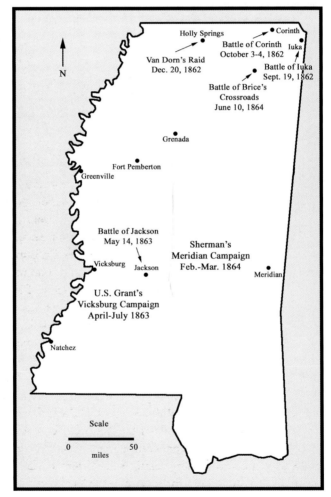

Military Activities in Mississippi, 1861-1865 (selected sites)

University Greys

After Mississippi seceded from the Union in 1861, students from the University of Mississippi at Oxford organized a volunteer company, the University Greys, under the command of William B. Lowry. The company was commissioned in April of 1861 and on May 1 left the campus and traveled to Corinth, where it became Company A of the 11th Mississippi Infantry Regiment. During the war the Greys participated in a number of battles in the Eastern theater but gained their greatest notoriety at Gettysburg. There, as part of Davis' Brigade, Heth's Division in A.P. Hill's Corps, the Greys suffered 100% casualties (14 dead and 17 wounded out of 31 who participated in the battle) during the Confederate defeat. Today, letters from members of the Greys are housed in the University of Mississippi's library, and the exploits of the company are immortalized in a large stained glass window in one of the buildings on campus.

ORGANIZING THE TROOPS

Against a backdrop of general confusion and uncertainty, Mississippi prepared itself for war during early 1861. After secession, Governor Pettus sent out the call for volunteer troops to be organized into four twelve-month regiments, but woefully underestimated the response to his order. Enlistment overwhelmed the initial demand for soldiers and soon more than eighty volunteer companies clamored to serve. Pettus ordered as many of these companies as possible to rendezvous points along the railroad at Corinth, Enterprise, Grenada, and Iuka. There the companies were organized into regiments, mustered briefly into state service, and then transferred to the Confederate Army. During the course of the war, Mississippians would serve in all the major campaigns involving the Army of Northern Virginia and the Confederacy's western armies, particularly the Army of Tennessee.

Because the volunteer companies were recruited locally, they contained many relatives and friends. Many of the men who volunteered for service in the local companies had grown up together, attended the same churches, and watched the sun rise and set on the same scenery all their lives. Their grand adventure in the Confederate Army represented an appealing extension of their neighborhoods, a community undertaking fortified by kinship and friendship ties. On average, most enlisted men were small farmers in their early to mid-twenties. The majority were unmarried and therefore better able to leave home for extended periods of time. Officers were usually somewhat older, prominent community leaders or men with some degree of military knowledge, either real or perceived. Throughout the South the organization of most Confederate infantry regiments followed the same pattern. A one-thousand-man regiment contained ten one-hundred-man companies from the same general geographic area.

CORINTH AND SHILOH

By the winter of 1861–1862 the Confederate West was in disarray. Following setbacks at Mill Springs, Kentucky and Forts Henry and Donelson in Tennessee, Union General Samuel R. Curtis defeated a Confederate force at Pea Ridge, Arkansas in early March. What had been the primary Confederate defense line in Kentucky collapsed for good as Albert Sidney Johnston, overall commander of the Confederate forces, abandoned its center at Bowling Green and fell back through Tennessee. With Kentucky and much of Tennessee gone, the Confederates scrambled to establish a new line of defense and to protect what had suddenly become one of the most strategically important points on the Southern map.

In 1862 Corinth, Mississippi had a population of about two thousand. With the collapse of Southern defenses in Kentucky, however, holding the small northeastern Mississippi town was crucial to the Confederate war effort. Corinth was a major railroad center. The Mobile and Ohio Railroad ran north–south through the settlement and the Memphis and Charleston—called by many the "vertebrae of the Confederacy"—ran east–west. Johnston eventually concentrated his army around Corinth and put out the call for more troops. Soldiers from various locations throughout the South answered the summons and by late March Johnston's army numbered about 40,000. Meanwhile, after his victory at Fort Donelson, Ulysses S. Grant moved freely through Tennessee, finally halting at Pittsburg Landing on the Tennessee River, where he went into camp with around

42,000 men. He planned to wait there for the arrival of Don Carlos Buell's 20,000-man Army of the Ohio. The combined Union force would then move south, attempt to capture Corinth, and if successful, plunge into the heart of Mississippi, dealing the Southern rebellion a mortal blow.

By early April the Confederate high command in Richmond was desperate to stop the Federal advance in the West. After studying reconnaissance reports of Grant's and Buell's movements, Confederate President Jefferson Davis wrote Johnston, instructing him to move quickly against the Union forces. Davis and his military advisors, including Robert E. Lee, believed that if Buell successfully united with Grant, their combined force would be difficult to fend off. With his object clearly defined, Johnston ordered his army north to face Grant. By the late evening of April 5 most of the Confederate Army was camped near Pittsburg Landing, about 25 miles north of Corinth, where Johnston announced to his subordinate commanders his plan to attack the next morning. Within distant earshot of the Confederate Army, Grant's soldiers were bedding down for the night. Their camp was on the western side of the Tennessee River near a small Methodist meeting house that would ultimately give the next day's events a name. The church was called Shiloh.

The Battle of Shiloh was among the first major bloodbaths that steered the course of the Civil War. During the two-day fight on April 6 and 7, 1862, Shiloh produced more casualties than all prior American wars combined. Around 13,000 Union troops fell along with a like number of Confederates. It was a savage, confused battle involving many men who were barely soldiers and who had never discharged a weapon at anything capable of returning fire. For the North, Shiloh was evidence that the Federal army would not easily defeat the Confederates. For the South, it gave painful notice that long-winded rhetoric about ideals and honor had little effect in the face of rifles, cannons, and bayonets. After the battle it was apparent to all that the Civil War would be an exceedingly bloody affair driven by resources, casualty counts, and the collective will of the participants. "Up to the battle of Shiloh," Grant later wrote, "I, as well as thousands of other citizens, believed that the rebellion against the government would collapse suddenly and soon if a decisive victory could be gained over any of its armies… but [afterwards] I gave up all ideas of saving the Union except by complete conquest." The Confederates won the first day's fight, but during the night Buell's troops arrived to reinforce Grant's army. The next day the Union army was victorious, forcing the Confederates into full retreat back to Corinth. Battered and bruised, the Confederates would surrender Corinth less than two months later; subsequent attempts to retake the railroad center ended in failure.

NORTH MISSISSIPPI

Later in the year Grant looked to move deeper into Mississippi and hopefully threaten Vicksburg on the bluffs overlooking the Mississippi River. As he took the offensive, Grant established a large supply depot and base of operations at Holly Springs, then concentrated most of his troops twenty miles to the south at Oxford. At the same time William T. Sherman led a Union force down the Mississippi. But two daring cavalry raids changed Grant's plans: Nathan Bedford Forrest, who would prove to be the scourge of Federal forces in the western theater for the rest of the war, moved into western Tennessee where he cut telegraph wires and disrupted Grant's extended supply lines. Then, in late December of 1862, Earl Van Dorn moved north from Grenada, targeting the Union supply depot at Holly Springs. His men circled behind Grant's army and destroyed more than a million dollars' worth of Federal supplies. At around the same time Sherman was having problems with his advance toward Vicksburg. He withdrew after the Battle of Chickasaw Bayou, north of the city. In the face of such opposition, Grant finally abandoned his plans and regrouped.

VICKSBURG

While discussing strategy with his military advisors in 1861, Abraham Lincoln emphatically stated that "Vicksburg is the key. The war can never be brought to a close until that key is in our pocket." For both the United States and the Confederacy, Vicksburg, Mississippi was a focal point from

Monument in the Vicksburg National Military Park honoring Brigadier General Lloyd Tilghman, C.S.A., killed at the Battle of Champion Hill in 1863. Image © Dreamstime.com

John C. Pemberton

John Clifford Pemberton, the general who defended Vicksburg from Ulysses S. Grant, was born in Philadelphia, Pennsylvania in 1814. A graduate of the United States Military Academy, Pemberton saw action in the Seminole War and served with distinction during the Mexican War. After the secession of the southern states in 1861, Pemberton's wife, a native Virginian, influenced his decision to fight for the South.

Pemberton was an able administrator and military politician, but he was uncomfortable in the role of combat commander. In part because of his "Yankee upbringing," controversy seemed to follow the general wherever he was assigned. Pemberton was given command of the Department of South Carolina and Georgia in March of 1862, but was soon relieved after those states complained that a Northern-born general might not look out for their interests. A few months later he was given command of the Department of Mississippi and East Louisiana and charged with protecting Vicksburg at all costs. Through 1862 Pemberton fended off Federal efforts to capture the city but was unable to halt Grant's 1863 siege of the river port. After the surrender of Vicksburg, Pemberton shouldered much of the public blame for the Confederate debacle amid false rumors that his Northern heritage had played a role in the capitulation. After the war, Pemberton settled in Warrenton, Virginia and later returned to Pennsylvania. He died in 1881 and was buried in Philadelphia.

the outset of the war. Situated on a large bluff overlooking the Mississippi River, Vicksburg controlled all traffic on the river. Lincoln and his generals knew that if they could wrest Vicksburg from the Confederates, then they could control the river and effectively split the Confederacy in two. Likewise, the Confederates realized that holding Vicksburg was essential to their cause. An attempt by the Federals to take the city in 1862 failed, but the following year Grant would move on Vicksburg again, this time successfully.

By the spring of 1863, Confederate forces in Mississippi were on the defensive, reacting in many cases frantically to rumored and actual Union troop movements. As Grant moved down the west bank of the Mississippi River in the early stages of what would be his successful campaign for

Vicksburg, Union Colonel Benjamin H. Grierson began his famous cavalry raid through much of the eastern half of Mississippi. Grierson's raid was designed to disrupt Confederate supply and communication lines that serviced Vicksburg and siphon off Confederate troops that could be used in Vicksburg's defense. In doing their duty, Grierson's men left a great deal of destruction in their wake as they passed through many Mississippi communities.

On April 30, 1863 the Union campaign for Vicksburg began in earnest as Grant and 23,000 Federals crossed the river into Mississippi at Bruinsburg, well below Vicksburg, and proceeded northeast toward Jackson. On May 1 the Federals secured their bridgehead across the river by defeating 6,000 Confederates at the Battle of Port Gibson. Grant then called for William T. Sherman and his troops, who were operating north of Vicksburg, bringing total Federal strength east of the Mississippi River to more than 40,000 men. John C. Pemberton, the Confederate general in charge of the region, had 30,000 troops at his disposal, but they were scattered in various detachments. Thus divided, they proved little impediment to Grant's swift progress. On May 12, a Confederate force under the command of Brigadier General John Gregg met defeat at the Battle of Raymond, and two days later Union troops drove the Confederates out of Jackson. Leaving William T.

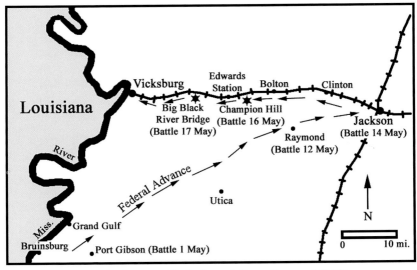

Vicksburg Vicinity, May-June 1863

Vicksburg National Military Park

One of Mississippi's most visited tourist attractions, Vicksburg National Military Park is located in the northeastern part of the city. It pays homage to the 47-day siege that made Ulysses S. Grant a hero, helped the Union win the Civil War, and pushed the Confederates inside the city to the brink of starvation. Self-guided driving tours of the park begin at the visitor center and meander sixteen miles through the former siege lines. Tour stops include a variety of entrenchments, monuments, the Vicksburg National Cemetery, in which nearly 17,000 soldiers are buried, and the U.S.S. *Cairo* naval museum. The park also plays host to reenactments, living history exhibits, and many community events during the year. In addition to the military park, the city of Vicksburg features numerous other historic sites related to the siege.

Sherman's corps in the Mississippi capital to destroy the city as a supply and transportation center, Grant turned his full attention west toward Vicksburg.

Union and Confederate troops clashed in the decisive battle of the Vicksburg campaign on May 16 at Champion Hill, near Edward's Station about halfway between Jackson and Vicksburg. There Grant concentrated 29,000 men against 23,000 under Pemberton. During several hours of bitter fighting, Champion Hill changed hands three times. The outnumbered Confed-erates eventually lost the field and retreated to the west, leaving behind twenty-seven cannons and hundreds of prisoners. The Confederates suffered 3,840 casualties at the Battle of Champion Hill to 2,441 for the Union. After another battle on May 17 at the Big Black River, Pemberton fell back into Vicksburg. Grant then made two unsuccessful attempts to take the city by direct assault. After suffering a great many casualties, the Federals settled in for a 47-day siege, during which the Confederate soldiers and civilians trapped in Vicksburg were reduced to eating horses, rats, and shoe leather. In addition, the Federals pounded the city with heavy artillery from the siege lines and from gun boats on the Mississippi. Pemberton finally surrendered unconditionally on July 4, 1863. Coupled with Robert E. Lee's defeat at Gettysburg, which took place at the same time, the fall of Vicksburg marked the beginning of the end of the Southern Rebellion. As for the citizens of Vicksburg, they would not celebrate Independence Day again until World War II.

MORALE & THE HOME FRONT

The year 1863 also marked the point at which the desertion rate among Mississippians in the Confederate army began to increase. Conditions at home contributed to more and more soldiers "going over to the hill" to end their service to the Confederacy. The original volunteers had signed on for a period of twelve months, firm in the belief that the war would be over before they completed their full tour of duty. They had left enthusiastic communities yet to know the deprivations of war, and had drawn strength from the encouragement that their communities provided. By the end of 1863, however, there were no more cheering crowds in Mississippi. Wartime difficulties had dampened enthusiasm for the war on the home front, which subsequently dampened the spirits of the men in the field. Accounts of hardships were widespread. "What awful times we are passing through," one Mississippi woman wrote, "It is just as much as we can do here to get enough to eat. I feel thankful for anything to live on." Letters from home that had once offered encouragement to the men were now filled with accounts of deprivations. The men had entered the service to defend their communities, but now their communities needed them back, and some soldiers acted accordingly.

Other men had grown disillusioned with the nature of the Confederate experience. The soldiers were originally volunteers, but through a mandatory conscription act their government had forced them into service for an extended period. According to one soldier, Confederate lawmakers had severely overstepped their bounds "when it comes to pressing the twelve month volunteers into service for two or more years without giving them the privilege of going home as free men." The government could not keep the

army adequately supplied, nor could it provide relief for the soldiers' families back home. Some deserters were simply tired of fighting a war that already seemed lost. Northern soldiers had defeated them in battle after battle and now tread confidently on Mississippi soil. For some soldiers who had entered the service as part of a community enterprise, it was the Federal occupation of their home state in 1863, not the fall of Richmond or the surrender at Appomattox, that marked the end of the war.

MERIDIAN

On February 3, 1864, William T. Sherman left Vicksburg and moved east with a force numbering around 20,000, intent on capturing Meridian. With the loss of Vicksburg, Meridian had become the last strategic Confederate-held location in Mississippi. The Mobile and Ohio Railroad crossed the Southern Railroad there and the city included a number of railroad shops, magazines, and hospitals. The Federals advanced across the center of the state in what proved to be a testing ground for the total war strategy that Sherman later employed during his famous march to the sea.

Although Confederate cavalry occasionally engaged Sherman's men, the Southerners could muster little resistance. Remnants of the Confederate forces in Mississippi fell back to the east as the Federals advanced. On February 14, Sherman's men entered Meridian without a fight. For five days they dedicated themselves to destroying the city until Sherman finally reported that "Meridian, with its depots, warehouses, arsenals, hospitals, offices, hotels, and cantonments no longer exists." During the course of the expedition across central Mississippi, Sherman's men destroyed 115 miles of railroad, 61 bridges, 20 locomotives, and countless other businesses and homes.

NATHAN BEDFORD FORREST AND
BRICE'S CROSSROADS

Despite the Confederate setbacks in Mississippi, famed cavalry general Nathan Bedford Forrest continued harassing Union forces in northern Mississippi and

William T. Sherman. Image courtesy of the Library of Congress.

Mississippi Casualties

Around 78,000 white Mississippians served the Confederate cause during the Civil War, and of those around 27,000 did not return. This represented a loss of approximately one quarter of the white male population aged fifteen and above in 1860.

Tennessee. In the summer of 1864 Union authorities realized that there would never be peace in the region unless they scattered or captured Forrest's command. In addition, General Sherman (who referred to Forrest as "the very devil") had begun his campaign for Atlanta and was worried that Forrest might hamper the effort by disrupting his extended supply lines. On June 1, 1864 Union troops led by Samuel J. Sturgis rode out of Memphis with orders to find and destroy Forrest's cavalry. Nine days later the Federals found Forrest at Brice's Crossroads near Baldwyn and a bloody, day-long battle ensued in the summer heat. Though outnumbered, the Confederates soundly defeated the Federals and forced them into a disorderly retreat. While Brice's Crossroads was a great personal victory for Forrest, Sherman's supply lines remained intact and Atlanta fell later in the year. Forrest survived the war to great glory and in 1867, while living in northern Mississippi, he became Grand Wizard of the Ku Klux Klan, a position he held for two years.

THE WAR'S END

While the defeats at Gettysburg and Vicksburg marked the beginning of the Confederate decline, the war carried on through the spring of 1865. In early April of that year the Confederate capitol at Richmond fell, and a few days later Robert E. Lee surrendered to Ulysses S. Grant at Appomattox Court House. On April 26 Joseph Johnston formally surrendered his western army to William T. Sherman in North Carolina, and after Jefferson Davis's capture in Georgia the Confederate government ceased to exist.

The Mississippi troops who had survived the war signed parole forms in 1865 and joined the ranks of what one Northern observer described as "poor homesick boys

African-American Soldiers

During the course of the Civil War many African Americans, including around 17,000 from Mississippi, fought for the Union. Initially confined to support duties, many of the soldiers eventually saw combat. Early African-American units fought with distinction during the Vicksburg campaign, prompting Ulysses S. Grant to write to Abraham Lincoln that "by arming the Negro, we have added a powerful ally." The participation of African-American troops during the war helped abolitionists argue for the extension of full civil rights to the African-American community. Conversely, the Confederates only authorized the arming of African-American troops out of desperation in March of 1865, just before the war's conclusion.

and exhausted men wandering about in threadbare uniforms, with scanty outfit of slender haversack and blanket role hung over their shoulder, seeking the nearest route home." They began their long trip back to Mississippi by any means possible. Some hitched rides on rickety rail cars or rode lank horses. Others simply walked. The men had abandoned their plows to leave home in defense of their state and new country, and had become hardened combat soldiers during the bloodiest war in American history. After the surrender, they returned home to become farmers once again and to help their communities recover from the ordeal. Their grand Confederate adventure had evolved into a grand Confederate tragedy, and their memories of the ordeal never faded.

6

RECONSTRUCTION, 1865–1877

Mississippi's surviving veterans returned home in 1865 to a state immersed in economic and social chaos. More than one-third of the 78,000 Mississippians who had participated in the "Confederate adventure" were dead, and many others were maimed for life. Farms, large and small, had deteriorated from neglect and hardly any money circulated. Debt was rampant. Five years after the war's conclusion the state would hold more than two million acres of land for non-payment of taxes. King Cotton had abdicated his throne, and by the end of the century the price of the fiber on which so many Confederate leaders had staked their hopes fell to four cents per pound. Emancipation quickly gave way to social turmoil that would not be effectively dealt with for another century. The turbulent Reconstruction period offered little relief, and once Democratic "Redeemers" wrestled control of the state away from the Republicans in 1876, their conservative fiscal policies made matters even worse. Fifteen years after Appomattox, the per capita income in Mississippi remained one of the lowest in the country at $82.

Property values also plummeted. Farmers worked less acreage than they had before the war and crop yields of both food crops and cotton were weak. Economic hardships affected planters and small farmers alike. In 1860 the average cash value of a farm in Holmes County, one of the wealthiest of the Mississippi counties, was $9,642, but by 1870, with many of the larger holdings broken up into smaller parcels, the average cash value per farm there had fallen to $1,208. Similarly, in Choctaw County, one of the state's poorest counties before the war, the average cash value per farm dropped from $1,754 in 1860 to only $320 a decade later.

Of course the war exacted more than just an economic toll on the veterans and their communities. In 1865 the former soldiers were tired, defeated, and many were crippled for life. For years the ghosts of men who should have still been living would haunt the Mississippi countryside. The communities that produced the soldiers were close-knit—almost everyone was "some kinda kin" to everyone else—and few families escaped the loss of a friend, neighbor, or loved one during the struggle. Many of the dead lay in unmarked graves scattered throughout the South, graves that their relatives would never visit.

Times were especially tough for Mississippi's 400,000 newly freed slaves. The war's outcome had given them their freedom but little else. They owned no property and had few possessions. Slavery had scattered many families, so one thing that the former slaves did try to do as quickly as possible was establish some sort of domestic life. Many freedmen wandered the roads of the state for months searching for lost relatives. Hundreds of slave marriages took place in the months immediately following the Civil War, legally sanctioning unions that had not been recognized during the antebellum period. The Federal government created the Freedmen's Bureau to distribute supplies to the needy and settle land claim issues, but it was never large enough in scope to provide a long range solution to Mississippi's (and the South's) many problems. For most blacks and whites alike there was scarce food, little medical care, and only threadbare hopes of some kind of recovery.

EARLY RECONSTRUCTION EFFORTS

Even before the war ended Abraham Lincoln put in place a lenient plan for "reconstructing" both the Southern states and the nation. His plan involved little more than most white Southerners taking a loyalty oath to the Union and accepting emancipation. Upon Lincoln's death, the presidency passed to Andrew Johnson, who also advocated a lenient plan. While both plans were designed to bring the Union back together as easily as possible, neither made any concrete provisions for civil rights for the newly freed slave. Johnson, in fact, was at times openly hostile to the African-American community. As a result, whites in Mississippi and the rest of the Southern states would quickly begin putting together state governments under what their political leadership considered favorable terms.

Andrew Johnson appointed a former Whig, William L. Sharkey, as provisional governor of Mississippi, and Sharkey called a constitutional convention that met in Jackson in August of 1865. During the convention, delegates actually argued over the abolition of slavery with some delegates claiming that Mississippi was still a sovereign state and could therefore not be forced to accept emancipation. More realistic voices prevailed, though, and the convention voted to abolish slavery by a count of 87–11. The convention also produced a new constitution and elections were scheduled for state and local officials. In October former Confederate General Benjamin G. Humphreys was elected governor, although he had to wait for his official pardon before taking office. The elections also produced a state legislature dedicated to reestablishing the old social order.

Once in office the newly elected legislature passed a series of controversial laws that were collectively known as the Black Code, which was designed to regulate the activities of the newly freed slaves and keep them subordinate. Viewed at the time as moderate legislation by many Mississippi whites, the Black Code did give the former slaves certain rights. They could testify in court when involved in litigation. They could own land under certain circumstances, and their marriages were legalized. However, the legislation also placed serious restrictions on the African-American community. Under many circumstances they could not rent or lease rural land, they could not own firearms, and they had to have a special license to do certain jobs. The legislature also passed vagrancy laws, under which former slaves could be arrested and, if they could not pay the required fine, "hired out" to their former masters or other whites. During Humphreys's tenure as governor (he served until 1867) federal troops were ordered to ensure the physical safety of the former slaves with as little interference as possible with Mississippi's civilian authorities. As a result, federal officials in Mississippi did little to counter the laws restricting freedmen, and despite subsequent claims to the contrary,

Rust College

Rust College in Holly Springs, Mississippi's first college for African Americans, was founded in 1866 by the Freedman's Aid Society of the Methodist Episcopal Church. Originally established on the site where Ulysses S. Grant's troops camped during the Civil War, the school was officially chartered in 1870 as Shaw University, in honor of Reverend S. O. Shaw, who made a $10,000 contribution to the institution. In 1882 the school's name was changed to Rust University as a tribute to Richard S. Rust of Cincinnati, Ohio, Secretary of the Freedman's Aid Society. In 1915 the school's name was again changed, this time to Rust College to better reflect the size of the school. During the 1960s the Rust campus was a hub of activity for the civil rights movement in northeastern Mississippi. Today, Rust College is an accredited four-year liberal arts college, and it remains the oldest historically black college in the state.

federal and civil authorities in the state generally coexisted peacefully.

Other Southern states followed Mississippi's lead with regard to how they should reestablish their old political and social order. The results generated loud protests from the North. Thousands of Federal soldiers had died during the Civil War, and it seemed to many as if the Southerners were attempting to turn back the clock and negate their defeat. The Southern states elected many Democrats and former Confederates to high office, men whom many Northerners still considered traitors. Congress countered in December of 1865 by refusing to seat the Southern Congressmen, which left the status of the new Southern governments unresolved. The Northern backlash also included calls for the South to extend full civil and political rights to the former slaves.

CONGRESSIONAL RECONSTRUCTION

In 1866 Congressional elections changed the course of Reconstruction. So-called Radical Republicans won solid control of Congress, effectively neutralizing Andrew Johnson as a political force. The Radicals immediately took over the administration of Reconstruction, and they refused to recognize the state governments that had been set up under the leadership of former Confederates. In March of 1867 Congress passed a series of Reconstruction Acts that reorganized the South. These acts created five military districts, each of which was placed under martial law. The Fourth Military District included Mississippi and Arkansas, with General E. O. C. Ord in command. Under the Reconstruction Acts, only those adult males in the state who swore the "ironclad oath" that they had never given aid to the rebellion against the United States could participate in creating a new state government. This initially excluded many Democrats and former Confederates from the process, and also allowed many freedmen to take an active role in Mississippi politics.

As a result, Mississippi was governed by Republicans for several years. Three general classifications of citizens made up the Republican Party in the state. First, there were those who came from outside the state to live in Mississippi and support Reconstruction policies, particularly those tenets dealing with the newly freed slaves. Their critics referred to them as "carpetbaggers" who had supposedly come into the state to take advantage of the situation and hopefully enrich themselves. Second, there were native white Mississippians who cooperated with Federal authorities in implementing Reconstruction policies. Critics referred to this group as "scalawags" who similarly wanted to use the post-war chaos to line their pockets. Finally, the largest block of Republican votes during the period came from the freedmen community, and a number of African Americans held public offices during the period.

A new constitutional convention convened in January of 1868. This convention included 26 "carpetbaggers," 33 "scalawags," and 16 African Americans, in addition to 29 white conservatives dedicated to preserving antebellum ways. Despite the fact that there were relatively few blacks at the convention, some conservative newspapers later

Adelbert Ames

Born in Rockland, Maine in 1835, Adelbert Ames graduated from the United States Military Academy in 1861 and served with distinction as a Federal officer during the Civil War. He was wounded at the First Battle of Bull Run and served as a division commander in a number of other major battles including Gettysburg, Cold Harbor, Petersburg, and Fort Fisher. For his efforts Ames was brevetted to major general in both regular and volunteer service. Assigned to Mississippi after the war, he became active in Republican politics. He was appointed military and provisional governor of the state in 1868, and after he resigned from the army two years later, the Republican-dominated legislature chose him to represent Mississippi as a United States Senator. Ames left Washington after being elected governor of Mississippi in 1873, but his political fortunes in Mississippi soon faded. Dedicated to helping the former slaves in their quest for full civil and political rights, Ames could not combat the massive white resistance to Reconstruction policies in the state. After the violent election season of 1875, during which Democrats gained a firm hold on the state legislature, Ames became the primary target for conservatives determined to rid the state of Republican rule. In 1876 he resigned as governor rather than face impeachment proceedings. Ames moved back to the North and in 1893 was awarded the Congressional Medal of Honor for his military service. The former Mississippi governor died in 1933 at the age of 97 as the last surviving full-rank general officer of the Civil War.

Cavalry detail at Gen. Adelbert Ames headquarters, taken between 1861–1869. Courtesy of the Library of Congress.

disparaged the meeting as the "Black and Tan Convention" and downplayed its accomplishments. The 1868 Mississippi Constitution produced by the convention was patterned after state constitutions in the North. Among other things, it declared that all persons residing in Mississippi, black or white, who were citizens of the United States were citizens of the state and had equal civil and political rights. The constitution also provided for a system of free public education and prohibited discrimination in the use of public facilities. Many of the provisions in the new Constitution provoked bitter opposition from conservatives and from many whites who soon regained their right to vote. Regardless, the Constitution was ratified, new elections were scheduled, and Mississippi officially reentered the Union in 1870 under Republican control.

The Republicans controlled Mississippi for approximately six years, during which time they repaired or rebuilt railroads, bridges, levees, and public buildings. The School Law of 1870 established Mississippi's first public school system, and the legislature passed a Civil Rights Act prohibiting discrimination in public places and on public conveyances. While African-American voters had influence during the period, African Americans never dominated Mississippi's government, as some would later claim. No African American was ever elected governor, nor were African Americans ever a majority in the legislature, and on the local level only one African American ever served as a mayor. However, even though Mississippi's Congressional delegation was always predominantly white, three African Americans briefly represented Mississippi in Washington during Reconstruction: Hiram R. Revels and Blanch K. Bruce in the United States Senate and John R. Lynch in the House of Representatives.

During the early 1870s a significant backlash against Reconstruction policies in Mississippi developed among conservatives, whose goal was to reclaim the state for the Democratic Party and to put in place, in one form or another, the social structure of the antebellum period. Conservatives formed political "White Men's Clubs" to appeal to the white masses and "Taxpayer Leagues" to protest the Republicans' fiscal policies. These groups served two purposes. They unified many white voters based on race and circulated anti-

Republican propaganda throughout the state. During the period groups such as the Ku Klux Klan, the Knights of the White Camellia, and the Sons of Midnight harassed and sometimes killed black and white Republicans alike. During local elections in 1874 and the statewide legislative elections of 1875 violence prevailed as the Democrats implemented the "Mississippi Plan," which generally involved race-based appeals to white voters and violence and intimidation to keep African Americans and white Republicans away from the polls. During the 1875 political season, vicious race riots broke out at Water Valley, Louisville, Macon, Columbus, Vicksburg, and other Mississippi communities. In Clinton more than twenty African Americans died during several days of rioting and many others were forced to flee the town. The statewide elections of 1875 represented a triumph for the Mississippi Plan. Widespread voter fraud and intimidation resulted in Democratic legislative victories in 62 of the state's 74 counties. Once seated, the new legislature impeached the Republican governor Adelbert Ames and "convinced" other Republican politicians to give up their offices. Although the official end of Reconstruction in the South would not occur until the election of President Rutherford B. Hayes in 1876 and the subsequent Compromise of 1877, the 1875 statewide elections marked the end of Reconstruction in Mississippi and the beginning of Democratic control of the state.

WHY RECONSTRUCTION FAILED

The Mississippi Plan became the blueprint used by other Southern states to rid themselves of Republican rule. Meanwhile, the federal government did nothing to combat the abuses. By the mid-1870s much of the Northern public had grown tired of the Reconstruction debate, which, in turn, caused many Northern politicians to lose interest. Civil rights for African Americans was not an issue that excited the Northern electorate, and a financial panic in 1873 made economic concerns a bigger priority in many circles. In general, Northern officials were more interested in industrial development than in committing significant resources to prop up state governments in the South against massive white resistance. They believed it more prudent to allow the Democrats back into Congress on their own terms, and then work with them within that body. After

Hiram Revels

Hiram Rhodes Revels, the first African American to serve in the United States Senate, was born to free parents in North Carolina in 1822. As a young man he worked briefly as a barber before leaving North Carolina to pursue his education. Revels attended school in Indiana and Ohio before graduating from Knox College in Bloomington, Illinois. In 1845 Revels was ordained as a minister by the African Methodist Church and traveled extensively, ministering to African-American congregations. He eventually settled in Baltimore, Maryland where he became pastor of a local church and principal of a school for African-American students. With the outbreak of the Civil War he helped organize Maryland's first two African-American regiments and eventually joined the Union Army himself as a chaplain. After the war Revels settled in Natchez, Mississippi where he involved himself in Republican politics. Taking a conciliatory attitude toward former Confederates, he served as an alderman in Natchez and as a state senator before the Mississippi Legislature chose him as a United States Senator. He served in Washington for just over a year, returning home in 1871 to become president of Alcorn College, now Alcorn State University, the first state-supported school for African Americans in Mississippi. He served in that position until 1873, and then again from 1876 to 1882. He later taught theology at Rust College while continuing his religious work. Revels died in 1901 while attending a church conference. Praised by whites and blacks alike, Hiram Revels was buried in Holly Springs.

Image of Hiram Revels provided by the Library of Congress.

four years of war and several years of Reconstruction the North was tired of fighting, and it gave the South back to the Democratic Party at the expense of the rights of the African-American community. Soon African Americans in Mississippi and in the rest of the South were legally excluded from the political system and officially segregated into a "separate but equal" world of their own.

Alcorn State University

Alcorn State University in Lorman, Mississippi's oldest state-supported historically black university, can trace its history back to the establishment of Oakland College in 1830. A Presbyterian School for whites, Oakland College closed during the Civil War and was unable to open again once the war ended. The college was sold to the state and in 1871 Alcorn University was opened on the property as an educational institution for African-American males. The school was named for James L. Alcorn, Mississippi's Republican governor at the time. Under the Morrill Land Grant Act the school became a land-grant institution in 1878 and its name was changed to Alcorn Agricultural and Mechanical College. The college admitted its first female students in 1903, and in 1974 it became Alcorn State University. Today Alcorn State University's eighty-nine buildings are situated on 300 acres, with an adjacent 1,456 acres devoted to agriculture and research.

RECONSTRUCTION MYTHS

A number of myths sprang up concerning Reconstruction, most of which were fabrications used for decades as propaganda to keep the Democratic Party in power and to ensure that Mississippi whites (and Southern whites in general) would never forget who "rescued" them from the evils of Republican rule. Even today many of these myths are wrongly accepted by some as fact. For instance, one of the great myths of Reconstruction involved the helpless South suffering great abuses under a prolonged military rule. In reality, military rule in the South only lasted about three years following the end of the war, and relatively few troops were stationed in the Southern states. In Mississippi the total number of troops in the state never exceeded 6,900, and by 1869, only four years after the Confederate surrender, there were only 716 federal soldiers in the entire state, an average of less than ten per county. Another myth alleged that the Reconstruction period was one of great political corruption in the South—that the carpetbaggers had entered the region to take advantage of the chaos, and that the scalawags had helped them plunder the helpless Southern states. In truth, in Mississippi there were some Republican officials who were corrupt and many who were not. Overall, there was no evidence that the Republican governments were any more or less corrupt than Democratic governments either before or after Reconstruction. In fact, during the four decades after the war there were three major embezzlement scandals involving state treasurers stealing funds. These took place in 1866, 1890, and 1902 when Democrats were in control. Finally, one lasting myth of the Reconstruction period held that the state governments in the South were dominated by African Americans who were only puppets of white Republicans and the Federal government. In fact, nowhere in Mississippi did blacks wield political strength equal to their voting strength. Blacks were never a majority in the state legislature, Mississippi never elected a black governor, and on the local level where the county sheriff was the most important position, only 12 of 74 sheriffs were African-American. In a state where African Americans represented roughly half of the population and 60 to 70 percent of the population in some counties, these figures signify considerable underrepresentation.

7

Into the 20th Century, 1877–1945

The Redeemers

Following Reconstruction, political power in Mississippi fell to a relatively small group of self-styled "Redeemers" who positioned themselves as saviors who had rescued, or "redeemed" the state from evil "Carpetbaggers, Scalawags, and their Negro agents." In some circles these men were known as "Bourbons," after the autocratic French royal family. Once the Redeemers took control of Mississippi, political progress stagnated. The state was part of the "Solid South," meaning solidly Democratic, and as such, debate over major political issues was significantly limited. There were fights within the party for power, but mainly these were struggles between individual personalities rather than struggles over competing policies or visions. For twenty years after Reconstruction only two men, John M. Stone and Robert Lowry, held the governor's office. Stone served from 1876 to 1882 and again from 1890 to 1896, while Lowry held office from 1882 to 1890. At the local level political leaders also took turns holding important positions.

The Redeemers were staunchly conservative. They cut state programs, which devastated many poor Mississippians, and were primarily committed to business and industry, particularly the railroads. While limited industrialization took place in some parts of Mississippi, the economic benefits were felt by only a few. By 1900 the per capita income in the state (and in the rest of the Deep South) was less than half that of the Northern states. The Redeemers' lowest priority seemed to be public education. In 1878 Mississippi Agricultural and Mechanical College (later Mississippi State University) was founded at Starkville, but the state's support for colleges and universities remained sparse. Overall, public education

The 1878 Yellow Fever Epidemic

The Mississippi State Board of Health was established in 1877, and a year later it was pushed to its limits as a yellow fever epidemic swept across the state. Thousands of Mississippians fell ill with the disease and there were many deaths. At the time no one knew how the disease was transmitted. When the fever appeared in a community, those with the means usually fled while those left behind cowered in their homes, afraid to venture outdoors. Yellow fever first appeared in August of 1878 in Grenada, where more than 350 of 2,000 residents died. Before a quarantine could be put in place the fever spread to other towns. Holly Springs in Marshall County was hit particularly hard, reporting more than 1,400 cases. The 1878 yellow fever epidemic ended in October when the first frost killed off most of the mosquitoes, but not before the disease affected forty-six towns and killed more than 3,000 Mississippians. The crisis led to much needed improvements in the state's health care system.

expenditures were one-tenth of the national average. Under the Redeemer regime teacher salaries dropped from an average of $56 per month for white teachers in 1875 to $28 per month in 1885. African-American teachers received even less.

The three most powerful politicians in the state during the Redeemer era were former Confederate military officers Edward Cary Walthall, James Zachariah George, and especially Lucius Quintus Cincinnatus Lamar. Of the three, Lamar was by far the most powerful and the most well-known nationally. A Georgian by birth, he moved to Mississippi in 1849 and entered politics. After Mississippi seceded from the Union, Lamar served as Confederate envoy to Russia, England, and France and emerged as a Congressman after the war—the first Democrat from Mississippi to return to Congress as Reconstruction ended. He later served as Secretary of the Interior under President Grover Cleveland and was appointed Associate Justice of the Supreme Court, serving there from 1888 until his death in 1893. Lamar was the acknowledged leader of the Democratic Party in Mississippi, and as such it was said that no Democrat could achieve high office in the state without his endorsement.

The Lost Cause

As the nineteenth century drew to a close, the seeds of Southern mythology regarding the service of the South's aging Confederate veterans began to take root. Defeated militarily, in the decades following 1865 the South struggled to vindicate the decisions that had led to secession and to an armed conflict that had cost so many men their lives. From the ashes of war and the turbulence of the Reconstruction period a cultural identity took shape, grounded in ideas and attitudes referred to collectively as the Lost Cause. Celebrations of the Lost Cause took many forms: annual civil and religious services honoring the Confederate dead, veterans' reunions, the deification of Confederate military leaders, the erection of Confederate monuments, and the emergence of groups such as the United Confederate Veterans (U.C.V.), United Sons of Confederate Veterans (U.S.C.V.), and United Daughters of the Confederacy (U.D.C.). Politicians on the stump used the language of the Lost Cause—language denoting moral superiority based on abstract notions of honor and chivalry—to garner votes, and ministers espoused Lost Cause virtues from the pulpit. State-approved textbooks "educated" generations of white Southern school children on the nature of the war as a noble struggle of principle, lost only in the face of superior Northern resources. For a century after the war the Lost Cause gave cultural authority to Confederate symbols, most prominently the "stars and bars" rebel flag. As they entered into the twentieth century, the states of the old Confederacy did their best to maintain this cultural identity by accenting the New South with many of the cosmetic trappings of an idealized Old South. From a practical standpoint, while salving the psychological wounds of defeat, embracing these symbols helped maintain both white supremacy and the political dominance of the Democratic Party in the region. Whenever the party was challenged, its leaders quickly and vigorously waved the rebel flag and used racially charged language to remind Mississippi's white voters of their responsibility to their "heritage."

While local support for the ex-soldiers took many forms in Mississippi, its most public manifestation involved annual gatherings of the surviving veterans, their families, and their friends. Reunions of surviving Confederate veterans became a sacred ritual of a post-war South struggling to justify war and defeat. The national or state organizations of the United Confederate Veterans sponsored many, but most were community events sponsored by local U.C.V. chapters or other civic groups. A few years after the war's conclusion, many of Mississippi's surviving veterans began holding informal reunions, and later more organized events after they established their U.C.V. chapters during the 1890s. The reunions were well attended by both the ex-soldiers and members of their communities, and were usually marked by speeches from prominent veterans and local politicians. More importantly, they served as a primary venue for the communal celebration of the Lost Cause and for the men to pay homage to the war itself as the central event in their lives.

By the time the generation of Mississippi males that had fought in the war began passing from the scene, their exploits as Confederate soldiers had already entered the realm of legend. In the South every veteran, regardless of rank, became a larger-than-life hero and every battle—large or small, won or lost—drew comparisons with the great battles of history. As the old soldiers disappeared, the communities in which they lived made efforts to preserve their memory forever. At hundreds of sites throughout the states of the old Confederacy, recognition of the veterans took the form of some type of statue or monument bearing appropriate names and inscriptions. The unveilings of these Confederate monuments were central rituals in the celebration of the Lost Cause, and were usually conducted as part of a grand ceremony replete with patriotic speeches and emotional appeals. Today these monuments still cast long shadows across courthouse squares throughout Mississippi, mute testament to the South's unique past.

CHANGES IN AGRICULTURE

In the decades after Reconstruction most of Mississippi's population made their living on small farms, and regardless of how hard they worked, most farmers remained poor. Cotton was still the state's primary cash crop, but a volatile market provided little long-term security for those who staked their livelihood on the fiber. The poor conditions under which most farmers toiled were aggravated by a new system of agriculture—one revolving primarily around tenancy and sharecropping—that developed throughout the South in the last quarter of the nineteenth century. During the period little money circulated in Mississippi, and the economy was tightly

Mississippi sharecropper. Photo by Jewis Wickes Hine. Courtesy of the Library of Conress.

*African-American sharecroppers faced racial prejudice in addition
to bleak economic prospects. Image courtesy of the Library of
Congress.*

controlled by Redeemer politicians and their allies. Many
farmers lost their land due to their inability to pay taxes or
retire other debts. Forced to survive on credit, they worked
land that they did not own, either as tenants or as
sharecroppers. The tenant usually owned his own tools
and farm animals and paid a flat rate to the landowner for
use of the land. At the end of the growing season he would
pay his rent with proceeds from the sale of his crop. The
sharecropper was at the bottom of the economic ladder. He
too had to pay for the use of the land he cultivated, but he

also had to purchase, on credit, all the tools and other necessities needed to produce a crop. His debt burden was greater and it was therefore more difficult for him to meet his obligations. One bad growing season, or one year of depressed cotton prices, could cause both tenants and sharecroppers to begin a cycle of debt from which they could never recover. Two bad years could be catastrophic. By 1900 around half of Mississippi's farmers worked land that they did not own, many permanently tied to large farms working off a perpetual debt. The situation effectively recreated the conditions of slavery for African Americans, who made up a large percentage of the sharecropper class, and as time wore on the system affected more and more whites, creating widespread dependency among the poor that would last for generations.

THE POPULIST MOVEMENT

During the 1890s one rival group temporarily challenged the political power of the Democratic Party in the state. At the time America's agricultural economy was in turmoil. Farm prices had dropped throughout the nation and the South, the country's poorest section, was hit particularly hard. As a result of their dire circumstances, white farmers in Mississippi tried to organize, first through the Farmer's Alliance movement of the 1880s and then as part of the Populist movement.

The Populist movement represented a more serious threat to the political establishment in all the Southern states in that it was an attempt to form a bona fide national third party. The Populists drew much of their strength from farms in the West and the South, and nationally the party promoted better conditions for all farmers, black and white. This position doomed the Populists in the South. In Mississippi one of the most important Populist leaders was Frank Burkitt, who ran unsuccessfully for United States senator and for governor during the 1890s. While no Populist candidate won election to national office from the state, Mississippi Populist candidates did manage to draw more than one-third of the vote from the Democrats, enough to frighten the Democratic leadership into action.

The Mississippi Democratic Party eroded Populist political strength through racial politics. The greatest fear of Mississippi's Redeemers and their heirs was the potential of the state's white farmers and black farmers uniting to overthrow the existing power structure. To combat this threat the Democrats evoked the legacy of the Civil War. Because Populism in part dealt with the rights of African-American farmers, the Democratic Party characterized the movement as some type of nefarious outside threat to the social order, linking it with "Negro Supremacy," just as they had done with the Republican Party during Reconstruction. They took great pains to remind Mississippi's white voters that the Democratic Party had fought against abolition before the war, had delivered the South from "Negro Rule" during Reconstruction, and that only the Democratic Party could protect white Mississippi from other outside threats. It was no coincidence that during this period state and local Democratic leaders promoted the raising of Confederate monuments throughout the state, and the legislature voted to place the Confederate "stars and bars" on the state flag. As a result, the Populist movement waned in Mississippi, the Democratic Party retained tight control of the state government for decades, and Mississippi remained one of the poorest states in the America.

THE RISE OF JIM CROW

During this same period the Democratic power structure took steps to permanently keep the races separated. After the Republicans abandoned Reconstruction, African Americans in Mississippi were left at the mercy of the white establishment, and in the last decades of the nineteenth century the state's political leaders took steps to deny them their rights as citizens. Mississippi, along with other Southern states, began implementing so-called Jim Crow laws, the goals of which were to keep the races separate and to keep African Americans subordinate. These laws barred African Americans from most public accommodations frequented by whites, such as hotels, theaters, restaurants, and public parks. They also called for separate railroad cars and segregated schools. In 1890 Mississippi produced a new constitution that included Jim Crow laws as well as voting provisions that took many African Americans and some poor whites out of the political process. "Let's tell the truth

Ida B. Wells (1862–1931)

Born to slave parents in Holly Springs, Mississippi, Ida B. Wells spent her adult life crusading for the rights of African Americans and women in the United States. After her parents died in a yellow fever epidemic, Wells raised her younger siblings while attending Rust College in Holly Springs. She later moved her family to Memphis, where she became a teacher and eventually co-owner of a local black newspaper. She began her career as a journalist writing editorials promoting equal rights for African Americans and crusading against lynching. Forced to leave Memphis after her life was threatened, she moved to Chicago where she married Ferdinand Barnett, an attorney and editor of one of Chicago's early African-American newspapers. Always outspoken, Wells continued her anti-lynching crusade and also took up the cause of women's suffrage. In 1906 she joined W. E. B. Dubois as part of the Niagara Movement, and three years later she was among the founders of the National Association for the Advancement of Colored People (NAACP). She remained one of the African-American community's strongest voices until her death in 1931.

if it bursts the bottom of the universe," one delegate to the Constitutional Convention stated during deliberations over the document. "We came here to exclude the Negro. Nothing short of this will answer." A two-dollar poll tax was put in place, as was a literacy clause that required potential voters to read and interpret a section of the new constitution before they were allowed to cast their ballots. In 1892 less than 10,000 of the state's 186,000 eligible African-American men were registered to vote, along with only 68,000 of the state's 120,000 eligible whites. The United States Supreme Court upheld these provisions in 1898 in *William v. Mississippi,* just two years after the landmark *Plessy v. Ferguson* case upheld the Jim Crow laws that kept the races "separate but equal" throughout the South.

The Turn of the Century

By the end of the twentieth century most of the old Redeemer group that had seized power following Reconstruction were passing from the scene, and a new generation of Democrats began to dominate state politics. After Mississippi adopted the primary system for electing state officers, new candidates had an opportunity to create a political base through widespread emotional appeals designed to sway the state's poorer white voters. James K. Vardaman quickly rose above his competition, building grassroots support by exploiting class and racial concerns among the masses. He pledged to make reforms that would aid poor whites, and he also assured his white audiences, in the most inflammatory language possible, that he was determined to keep the African-American community subordinate. His platform included advocating the repeal of the Fifteenth Amendment, which was designed to protect black voting rights, and the modification the Fourteenth Amendment, defining citizenship so that it did not include African Americans, whom Vardaman claimed were not fit to be citizens. He also said that lynching was justified in some cases, depending on the offense. Vardaman knew his audience was poor, that they lived in economic insecurity every day of their lives, and that one of their primary fears was of competing with African Americans on a social and economic level. He exploited his constituents' fears and was revered by many poor white Mississippians as the "Great White Chief." Vardaman's demagogic rants helped him win the governor's race in 1904. Ironically, once his campaign was over and he was safely inaugurated, Vardaman did little to implement policies that directly hurt the African-American population in Mississippi. Considered a progressive governor despite his racial excesses, he sponsored various reforms legislations dealing with child labor, textbooks for schools, and improvements in the state's prison system, but had only limited success in effecting long-term change. He later represented Mississippi in the United States Senate but fell out of favor with Mississippi voters after clashing with Democrat Woodrow Wilson and opposing America's entry into the First World War.

Vardaman and those politicians that followed him made much out of pledging to help the state's poor white

The Teddy Bear

One of America's all-time favorite children's toys, the teddy bear, got its name from an event that took place in Mississippi. In 1902 President Theodore Roosevelt visited the state in an effort to clear up a boundary dispute between Mississippi and Louisiana. As the story goes—and there are several versions—during his spare time the President went hunting in Sharkey County but could scare up little game. At one point someone captured a large bear and tied it to a tree for Roosevelt to shoot. When he came upon the bear he refused to kill the defenseless animal and ordered it released. Press reports of the event inspired Clifford Berryman, a Washington political cartoonist, to draw his interpretation of the story. Berryman's cartoon, showing Roosevelt and the bear, ran in the *Washington Post* with the caption "drawing the line in Mississippi," a reference to both the boundary dispute and his refusal to shoot the defenseless animal. Berryman took artistic license with his subject by depicting a small, innocent-looking bear cub with the President rather than the larger adult animal. The cartoon, in turn, inspired enterprising toy makers to create the "teddy bear," which quickly became popular with the public. In 2002 the Mississippi Legislature commemorated the 100th anniversary of Roosevelt's hunt by making the teddy bear the official state toy.

farmers, but they did little to improve Mississippi's fiscal climate. In 1908 the boll weevil invaded the state, destroying most of the cotton crop and creating even more problems for the farm population. For a time, the state's economy took a slight upturn as the lumber industry boomed. Corporations, most from outside the state, employed thousands of Mississippians, and the state became one of the nation's leading lumber producers. However, by 1920 more than half of the state's virgin forests had disappeared, leading to major soil erosion problems in many areas. Because Mississippi's population remained poor, rural, and uneducated, other industries failed to grow in the state. Tenancy and sharecropping generated an increasing debt burden for many farmers and general hard times prevailed.

WORLD WAR I AND THE GREAT DEPRESSION

In 1917 Mississippi's governor Theodore Bilbo cancelled the state's centennial celebration due to the Unites States' involvement in World War I. Most Mississippians supported the war effort and the state contributed more than 60,000 troops. Thousands of American soldiers trained at Camp Shelby, near Hattiesburg, and at Payne field, an aviation camp near West Point. Mississippi also contributed seven general officers to the effort. The war helped Mississippi's economy by creating a demand for raw materials, particularly cotton, but following the armistice in 1918 the economy settled back into a familiar pattern. Through the 1920s Mississippi remained one of the nation's poorest states, and the condition of most Mississippians was made even more tenuous with the onset of the Great Depression. With the collapse of the national economy, the demand for manufactured goods dried up as unemployed workers throughout the country had little or no disposable income. This, in turn, lessened demand for raw agricultural products, particular cotton, which had provided most Mississippi farmers with at least a meager income. More farmers lost their land, becoming sharecroppers mired in an unending cycle of debt. By 1932 the per capita income of Mississippi's population was $132. That same year, during Governor Mike Connor's administration, the state passed one of the first sales taxes in the nation, increasing the burden on Mississippi's poor. As Mississippi's political leadership did little to provide relief to their constituents, the state continued wasting tax money by supporting separate school systems, one for whites and one for African Americans. The period also saw Mississippi's four major public universities, the University of Mississippi, Mississippi Agricultural and Mechanical College (now Mississippi State University), Mississippi State Teachers College (now the University of Southern Mississippi), and Mississippi State College for Women (now Mississippi University for Women) lose their accreditation.

Mississippi Agriculture and Forestry Museum

One of Mississippi's most visited tourist attractions, the Mississippi Agriculture and Forestry Museum opened in 1983 in Jackson with the mission of preserving and educating visitors about Mississippi's agricultural heritage. The large complex includes a working farm reconstructed with vintage buildings from around the state. The farm, which produces a variety of crops, has been restored to its 1920s appearance with a farmhouse, barn, storehouse, smokehouse, buggy shed, and other outbuildings. After touring the farm, visitors can walk the streets of an entire town, recreated with period (circa 1920s–1930s) structures moved to the site from all over the state, including a general store, church, doctor's office, blacksmith shop, filling station, and working cotton gin. The museum grounds also include an exhibition hall, with 17,500 Native American artifacts, and the National Agricultural Aviation Museum, which honors early pilots who pioneered crop dusting during the 1920s.

While many farmers felt economically trapped in Mississippi, others did not. One of the significant social changes brought on by World War I and the years that followed was the migration of hundreds of thousands of African Americans from the rural South to the North. They migrated for two simple reasons. First, they were fleeing the South's poverty and racism, and second, the North's industrial cities held job prospects, particularly factory jobs left behind by millions of men who had joined the war effort overseas. The migration continued after the war, and the period saw a dramatic growth of urban African-American communities in cities such as New York, Chicago, Cleveland, and Detroit. While the number of immigrants decreased once the war ended, the northward movement of African Americans, including

Piney Woods School

Situated on 2,000 acres in rural Rankin County, Piney Woods School is the largest historically black boarding school in the nation. Dr. Laurence C. Jones founded Piney Woods in 1909 with two students and a vision of creating a coeducational boarding institution for African-Americans. In his own words, he hoped to provide students in his care with a "head, heart, and hands" education. The first campus building was an abandoned sheep shed that was cleaned, repaired, and whitewashed by Jones himself. Through his constant attention and hard work the school survived against the odds, and today it boasts 300 students from all over the United States as well as from Africa and the Virgin Islands. Ninety-eight percent of Piney Woods students in grades 7–12 go on to attend college.

thousands from Mississippi, continued for several decades, peaking again as a result of World War II. Because of this migration, the census year 1940 marked the first time since 1830 that whites outnumbered blacks in Mississippi, albeit only slightly. The movement ultimately changed the dynamics of national politics, and of politics in Mississippi.

THE 1927 FLOOD

In 1927 one of the greatest natural disasters ever to take place in the United States struck Mississippi, adding to the state's woes. Beginning in the late summer of 1926, heavy rains swelled the Mississippi River to the point where it flowed over its levees, flooding much of the Mississippi Delta. The flood covered almost 3 million acres of land, much of which was devoted to agriculture—primarily cotton plantations owned by whites and worked by African Americans. The rushing water displaced more than 185,000 Mississippians and damaged or destroyed more than 100,000 structures. An entire crop year was lost, as were thousands of farm animals. The Red Cross established refugee camps to aid the homeless, and other forms of

Population Statistics

Mississippi Population by Race 1910–1950 (% of total population)

Year	White	Black
1910	786,111 (43.7)	1,009,487 (56.2)
1920	853,962 (47.7)	935,184 (52.2)
1930	998,077 (49.7)	1,009,718 (50.2)
1940	1,106,327 (50.7)	1,074,578 (49.2)
1950	1,188,632 (54.6)	986,494 (45.3)

assistance poured in from outside the state. However, much of the relief was distributed on the basis of race. Although three quarters of the Mississippians affected by the flood were African-American, Red Cross aid was often channeled to whites only. As the disaster unfolded, white women and children were quickly taken to safety while much of the African-American community was forced into refugee camps, tightly administered by whites amid fears that removing them would deplete the Delta's labor force. The crisis eventually passed, but the region's landscape was forever altered.

THE NEW DEAL

Desperate for economic relief, most Mississippians initially welcomed Franklin D. Roosevelt's New Deal and faithfully supported the President and his programs. The common man looked to Roosevelt as a savior, while the state's political establishment was pleased to have a Democrat in the White House. However, many of Mississippi's public officials would eventually sour on the Roosevelt presidency. As more New Deal legislation worked its way through Congress, it became apparent that Roosevelt's national agenda was designed to aid whites and African Americans alike. Legislation dealing with fair labor practices and anti-lynching laws were unacceptable to a political establishment in Mississippi that rested squarely on a foundation of racial segregation. The tension between the Roosevelt administration and Mississippi's Democratic leadership was further strained as Eleanor Roosevelt spoke out publicly of her concern for the rights of the African-American

Large house moved off its foundation following the Mississippi flood of 1927. Photo copyright Ewing, Inc.

Ewing Inc
M-137
9-18-27

community, many of whom continued to migrate into Northern cities where they could vote. These events signaled the beginning of a major split between the national Democratic Party and Democrats in the Southern states. In the end, Roosevelt's New Deal did little to help most Mississippians. Any benefits stemming from federal programs usually accrued to wealthy landowners who exercised influence on the disbursement of federal funds in the state. One of the few positive aspects of Mississippi politics during the New Deal era was the election of Hugh White as governor. White took office in 1936, dedicated to helping Mississippi expand its industrial base. He launched his "Balance Agriculture with Industry" (BAWI) program devoted to attracting industry to Mississippi through tax breaks and local financing plans. One of the first major corporations that relocated to Mississippi under the program was Ingalls Shipbuilding Corporation, which came to Pascagoula in 1938. While other industries did not immediately flock to the state, White's initiative paved the way for future industrialization.

WORLD WAR II

Just as they had done during World War I, Mississippians lent their wholehearted support to the war effort after the Japanese attack on Pearl Harbor. More than 230,000 Mississippians served in the armed forces during World War II, with six earning the Congressional Medal of Honor. Because of its mild climate, Mississippi served as a training ground for hundreds of thousands of servicemen from all over the country. Camp Shelby was expanded to include over 300,000 acres and housed as many as 75,000 soldiers at any given time. On the Gulf Coast, Keesler Field (later Keesler Air Force Base) also trained hundreds of thousands of servicemen. At full capacity Keesler housed 69,000 soldiers, making it the largest airbase in the world at the time. In addition to Camp Shelby and Keesler Field, smaller installations were scattered throughout the state. In all, approximately one million men and women were given their military training in Mississippi between 1941 and 1945.

Mississippians celebrated the allied victory along with the rest of the nation, and then set about the task of readjusting to peacetime and a new, modern era. World

The New Capital

By the end of the nineteenth century Mississippi's state house in Jackson was obsolete. As a result, plans were made to construct a new, more elaborate capitol building to house the state's government. The "New Capitol," as it came to be known, was constructed between 1901 and 1903 at a cost of just over one million dollars, with much of the funding for the project coming from back taxes owed to the state by the Illinois Central Railroad. Renowned architect Theodore C. Link of St. Louis designed the building as an outstanding example of Beaux Arts Classicism architecture. More than 20,000 Mississippians attended ceremonies dedicating the capitol on June 3, 1903, Jefferson Davis's birthday. The festivities included a grand parade through the city and speeches by state and local dignitaries. Between 1979 and 1982 the already impressive building was renovated at a cost of nineteen million dollars, and today it remains open to the public for free tours.

War II changed the state's social, economic, and political environment. During the war and the years that followed, Mississippi's economy improved. The period saw an overall expansion of industry, mechanization in agriculture, and increased crop diversification. A whole way of life began passing from the scene as thousands of farmers moved from the countryside into the state's cities and towns. The participation of thousands of African Americans in the war effort would ultimately lead to the call for racial equality at the national level, which in turn would help give rise to the civil rights movement. World War II shattered the status quo in Mississippi, paving the way for a period of great change and great turbulence.

8

INTO THE MODERN ERA, 1946–

THE POSTWAR ECONOMY

The end of World War II ushered in a new era in Mississippi. The war created an economic boom in the state, helping many struggling farmers out of debt and onto their feet. Increased agricultural production and prices, along with the increased production of manufactured goods, brought a degree of prosperity to a state that had known only economic despair since the end of the Civil War. Farmers still grew cotton, but the crop was no longer "king" in Mississippi. After 1945 more and more farmers grew soybeans, corn, wheat, and rice. Livestock and poultry production increased dramatically. The end of the war also marked the beginning of mechanization in agriculture. The tractor, first introduced in small numbers to Mississippi during the 1920s, became a mainstay of the farm, putting the horse and mule permanently out to pasture. By the 1950s larger farms were using mechanical cotton pickers and other machines that increased efficiency and also eliminated the need for much of the state's farm labor. Tenancy and sharecropping disappeared, but not without a price. Replaced by machines, many of Mississippi's poorest farmers were forced to abandon the land and seek work in towns or out of state. In the three decades after the end of the war Mississippi farmers almost doubled their incomes from crops and livestock, but most of the money accrued to larger producers who had the funds to purchase expensive farm equipment. As a result, the number of small family farms declined and not everyone shared in the agricultural success.

Some farmers who could not make a living on the land were able to find factory jobs as Mississippi began to industrialize. Ingalls shipyard in Pascagoula became a

Pilgrimages

In 1931 the Mississippi State Federation of Garden Clubs held its annual meeting in Natchez, where members organized tours of the city's antebellum mansions. The visits to the mansions generated so much enthusiasm that the following year Mrs. J. Balfour Miller organized another tour. Her connections with various media throughout the South and the rest of the country allowed her to widely publicize the week-long event. The response to the first Natchez Pilgrimage in 1932 exceeded all of Mrs. Miller's expectations, and it became an annual spectacle celebrating an idealized version of the Old South. Recognizing the economic benefits of such an event, other cities around the South organized their own pilgrimages, complete with hoop-skirted tour guides who spoke with pronounced southern drawls. Today, in addition to Natchez, the cities of Vicksburg, Columbus, Holly Springs, Port Gibson, Aberdeen, Raymond, and the Gulf Coast all host annual pilgrimages that draw thousands of tourists to Mississippi.

major industrial employer that swelled the population of the Gulf Coast. Its success inspired other parts of the state to actively pursue industry, and by the end of the 1960s Mississippians employed in manufacturing outnumbered those in agriculture for the first time. Because of its mild climate Mississippi also benefited economically from the maintenance of military installations within its borders, most notably Camp Shelby near Hattiesburg and air force bases near Biloxi and Columbus, all of which continued training soldiers after the war. However, despite increased agricultural production, an increased industrial payroll, and the economic benefits of the state's military installations, Mississippi per capita income remained among the lowest in the nation due to a disparity of wealth between the "haves" and the "have nots."

THE "DIXIECRAT" REVOLT AND POLITICAL CHANGE

The postwar years also saw a dramatic change in Mississippi's political landscape, particularly during the 1948 presidential election season. Moral concerns and political pressure from the growing African-American voting population in the North led the national Democratic Party into the arena of civil rights. In October of 1947 President Harry Truman's Committee on Civil Rights promoted a program to guarantee the rights of African Americans in the United States. In response, Mississippi's governor Fielding Wright joined a chorus of Southern politicians who spoke out vehemently against the Committee's proposals, calling them an attack on the South's "traditions and institutions." When the national Democratic Party nominated Harry Truman for reelection as president in 1948 and adopted a platform addressing civil rights concerns, Mississippi's delegates left the convention and joined other Southerners at a separate meeting to nominate their own candidates. The southern ticket undertook the presidential race using the banner of the States' Rights Party. Nicknamed the "Dixiecrats," the new party nominated Strom Thurmond of South Carolina for president and Mississippi's Wright for vice president. It also adopted a platform condemning the national Democratic Party's stance on civil rights.

Truman won the election, but the race marked the beginning of the end of the solidly Democratic South. As national concerns over civil rights increased, the national Democratic Party associated itself with the movement, alienating many Southern Democrats and helping to create, for the first time since Reconstruction, a viable Republican Party south of the Mason-Dixon Line. Democrat Adlai Stevenson carried Mississippi in 1952, but the state's voters turned out in significant numbers (around 40%) for Republican Dwight D. Eisenhower. In 1964, 87% of Mississippi's voters—who were still primarily white—cast ballots for ultraconservative Republican Barry Goldwater over fellow Southerner Lyndon Johnson, who as president began promoting a civil rights agenda. Segregationist George Wallace carried Mississippi as an Independent in 1968, and for the rest of the twentieth century, with the exception of

Jimmy Carter's narrow victory over Gerald Ford in 1976, no Democratic presidential candidate would carry the state.

BROWN V. BOARD OF EDUCATION

On May 17, 1954 the United States Supreme Court overturned the 1896 *Plessy* decision that had legalized segregation. In *Brown v. Board of Education*, a case dealing with the inequities of segregated schools, the justices ruled unanimously that "separate educational facilities are inherently unequal." The ruling marked the beginning of the end of legal segregation in the South and was a bombshell in Mississippi. The state's stunned political establishment scrambled for a strategy to fight the decision, and the editor of Mississippi's most influential newspaper predicted bloodshed. The state's senior United States senator, ultra-conservative James O. Eastland, declared his belief that the decision was the result of some type of nefarious conspiracy, probably associated with communism, and even the state's more moderate voices pledged to fight the decision using any means necessary. Among the first steps taken by the state legislature were bills abolishing compulsory school attendance and passage of a variety of resolutions lauding states' rights and condemning federal interference in state affairs. Throughout the state, threats increased against African Americans viewed as too "outspoken" on the issue.

JAMES MEREDITH AT OLE MISS

In 1962 one of the watershed events of the civil rights era in Mississippi took place as James Meredith, a 29-year-old African-American air force veteran, prepared to enter the University of Mississippi (Ole Miss). Meredith had applied for admission the previous year, but he was rejected after the registrar's office discovered that he was not white. After a protracted legal battle the Fifth Circuit Court of Appeals ruled that the University had "engaged in a carefully calculated campaign of delay, harassment, and masterly inactivity" based on Meredith's race. The court ordered Ole Miss to admit Meredith immediately. In response, Mississippi's segregationist governor Ross Barnett went on statewide television and vowed to resist the ruling.

On the afternoon of September 30, 1962 a crowd opposing Meredith's admission to the University gathered on campus and began harassing United States marshals who had been brought in to keep order. Some members of the mob were from Mississippi, while many others were segregationists from neighboring states. They began throwing rocks and bottles and overturning nearby cars and trucks and setting them on fire. As the sun set, events spiraled out of control, and marshals fired tear gas into the crowd. Bullets began to fly and a full scale riot ensued, during which two people were killed and many others were hurt. One hundred and sixty marshals were injured, including twenty-eight who were shot during the fracas. Order was restored only after President Kennedy nationalized the Mississippi National Guard and sent in an additional 20,000 federal troops. At 8:00 AM the morning after the riot, James Meredith officially broke the color barrier at the University of Mississippi by completing the registration process.

THE EARLY CIVIL RIGHTS MOVEMENT

After the *Brown* decision the civil rights movement began in earnest, as did a period of turbulence in Mississippi the likes of which had not seen since the Civil War. Mississippi's political and economic leaders pledged "massive resistance" to the movement, echoing the sentiments of their counterparts in other Southern states. Several organizations, some private and others state-sponsored, were created to fight desegregation. In the Delta town of Indianola, farmer Robert Patterson organized local white business and community leaders into the state's first Citizens' Council, a segregationist group. By November of 1954, just six months after the *Brown* decision, over one hundred Council chapters were operating in the state and the movement claimed over 20,000 members. The Citizens' Councils were made up primarily of upper and middle class whites who had the means to exert economic pressure on any African Americans who involved themselves in the civil rights movement. Blacks who signed petitions supporting the *Brown* decision and calling for immediate school desegregation found themselves out of work or unable to get credit at local banks. Those involved with the increasingly vocal National Association for the Advancement of Colored People (NAACP) might not be able to purchase necessities at white-owned stores. This type of pressure successfully stifled the movement in many places, at least for a time. In 1956 the Mississippi Legislature created the State Sovereignty Commission "to prevent encroachment upon the rights of this and other states by the Federal Government." The Commission included state political and civic leaders and employed private detectives to secretly "investigate" anyone associated with the civil rights movement. Many of the Commission's activities were coordinated with the Citizens' Councils.

Of course not all pressure was economic. The civil rights movement in Mississippi also generated a great deal of violence. In some parts of the state the Ku Klux Klan was revived to terrorize African Americans and harass any whites perceived as having sympathy for the movement. In Belzoni, Reverend George Lee, an NAACP leader, died in a car accident after his automobile was fired on. Lee's friend and fellow NAACP worker Gus Courts was shot and almost killed as he tended his grocery store. No one was ever charged in either crime. In Poplarville, Mack Charles Parker, an African American accused of assaulting a white woman, was dragged from a local jail and lynched by a group of white men, none of whom were ever held accountable for their actions.

Several race-related murders in Mississippi received major national attention during the civil rights era. In 1955 Emmett Till, a 14-year-old African American boy, came south from Chicago to visit relatives in Money, a small town in the Delta. Till disappeared shortly after supposedly whistling at a white woman. His battered body, wrapped in barbed wire and weighted down, was later recovered from the Tallahatchie River. Two men were acquitted of the murder, but their trial focused national attention on Mississippi's racial problems. During the late 1950s and early 1960s, World War II veteran Medgar Evers was Mississippi's NAACP field secretary, and as such was heavily involved in voter registration and various educational programs for African Americans in the state. On June 12, 1963 a sniper killed Evers with a single shot in the back from a high-powered rifle. The NAACP's chief representative in Mississippi fell in his driveway, having just arrived home after watching a televised address by President John F. Kennedy on racial justice. Evers's killer would not be forced to pay for his crime for more than a quarter-century. A year after Evers's death, three civil rights workers, Michael Schwerner, James Chaney, and Andrew Goodman, disappeared in Neshoba County as they drove back from investigating reports of an African-American church burning. Their disappearance touched off a massive search and several weeks of national publicity before their bodies were finally found buried in an earthen dam. Several men with Ku Klux Klan ties, including local law enforcement officers, were implicated in their deaths.

Schwerner, Chaney, and Goodman were participating in a large project sponsored by the Council of Federated Organizations (COFO), a sometimes uneasy alliance of various civil rights groups including the NAACP, the Southern Christian Leadership Conference (SCLC), the Student Non-Violent Coordinating Committee (SNCC), and the Congress of Racial Equality (CORE). The effort, dubbed the Mississippi Summer Project of 1964, brought into the state hundreds of volunteers, both white and black, from around the country. Volunteers organized "freedom schools" to educate the African-American community with regard to their rights as citizens and led voter registration drives. As a result, Klan activity increased and violence escalated. In addition to the Schwerner, Chaney, and Goodman murders, other civil rights workers—dubbed "outside agitators" by some Mississippi whites—were beaten, shot, or arrested, and dozens of churches and other buildings were bombed.

THE FREEDOM DEMOCRATIC PARTY

COFO workers also set up a political organization, the Mississippi Freedom Democratic Party (MFDP), to challenge Mississippi's political establishment. In August of 1964, as the national Democratic Convention approached, Mississippi Democrats made plans to send their all-white delegation to the gathering. In response, the MFDP protested and petitioned the credentials committee of the national Democratic Party, claiming that the delegation chosen by Mississippi Democrats did not accurately represent the people of the state because it did not included any African Americans. They argued that instead of seating the all-white group, the convention should seat a biracial coalition of MFDP members. The credentials committee refused to seat the integrated delegation but the national press covered the struggle, giving even more publicity to the state of political affairs in Mississippi and in the South in general.

Fannie Lou Hamer

Born in Montgomery County in 1917 as the youngest of twenty children in a Mississippi sharecropping family, Fannie Lou Hamer gained national attention as a civil rights activist during the 1960s. Hamer married in 1944 and moved to Ruleville, where she worked as a field hand on a local plantation. She was later promoted to timekeeper when it was discovered that she could read and write. In 1962 the civil rights movement arrived in Ruleville and Hamer immediately became involved, registering to vote and losing her job as a result. She worked tirelessly for the Student Non-Violent Coordinating Committee (SNCC) and was a founder of the Freedom Democratic Party. As the Party challenged the state's regular Democratic delegation at the 1964 Democratic Convention, Hamer went on television and told her story of the abuse she had suffered a year earlier at the hands of the police in Mississippi after she had tried to use a local bus station. In her community she was a larger-than-life character and a tireless worker to improve conditions for Mississippi's impoverished. During the 1970s Ruleville held "Fannie Lou Hamer Day" in recognition of her work and she also received honorary degrees from Tougaloo College, Shaw University, Morehouse College, Columbia College, and Howard University. Fannie Lou Hamer's struggles ended in 1977 when she succumbed to cancer.

Fannie Lou Hamer at the Democratic National Convention, Atlantic City, New Jersey, August 1964. Photo by Warren K. Leffler.

Hurricane Camille

In August of 1969, one of the most intense hurricanes on record slammed into the Mississippi Gulf Coast, changing it forever. When Hurricane Camille came ashore its winds measured more than 200 miles per hour. It destroyed homes, businesses, and churches while tossing trees, telephone poles, and vehicles through the air as if they were toys. A twenty-foot tidal surge lifted huge barges and smaller crafts from their moorings and deposited them miles inland, on top of homes in some cases. Though some evacuation took place along the coast, many people stayed, underestimating the storm's strength. One hundred and forty three people perished, some while attending "hurricane parties." The morning after Camille struck, debris of all kinds littered the Gulf Coast. As it moved north the storm weakened, but it continued wreaking havoc through Tennessee and into the Appalachians, where high winds and massive flooding accounted for over a hundred more deaths. Hurricane Camille was one of only two Category 5 hurricanes on record to make landfall along the United States coastline. The final losses were staggering. The storm killed two hundred and fifty six people, displaced thousands, and the monetary damages totaled more than $1.4 billion.

Change

By the end of the 1960s it was evident that the old ways were dying out in Mississippi. The perseverance of those involved in the civil rights movement, along with evolving attitudes among many whites, brought about change that would have seemed impossible to achieve just two decades earlier. Business leaders began to realize that racial strife retarded Mississippi's economic growth, and that it was difficult to attract industry to a state filled with so much turmoil. Most Mississippians, black and white, tired of conflict, and an era of violence and uncertainty gave way to an era of transition and peace. Beginning with the 1969–1970 academic year, school desegregation took place across Mississippi with few incidents. While private all-white academies were established in some areas to circumvent desegregation, the vast majority of Mississippi's children began attending integrated public schools. At the university level James Meredith opened the door for other African Americans, and soon all of the state's institutions of higher learning were integrated. In 1976 popular Ole Miss football star Ben Williams, an African American, was elected by his fellow students as "Colonel Rebel," the most coveted social honor on the Ole Miss campus. Since then African-American students have served as president of the university's student body. While the state's racial problems did not completely disappear, Mississippi in many ways emerged in the last quarter of the twentieth century as a model for positive race relations when compared to some other areas of the country.

Smith Robertson Museum

Located on Bloom Street in downtown Jackson, the Smith-Robertson Museum houses an impressive array of artifacts related to Mississippi's African-American community. Named for the capital city's first African-American aldermen, the museum is housed in a building that served as Jackson's first public school for African-American children. The school closed in 1971 during public school desegregation but the building, constructed in the 1920s, was placed on the National Register of Historic Places in 1977. The museum opened in 1984, and its collection includes artifacts related to civil rights leaders Medgar Evers, Aaron Henry, James Meredith, Claire Collins Harvey, and many others. Noted African-American author Richard Wright attended the Smith Robertson School from 1923 to 1925.

During the 1970s single-party politics in Mississippi also ended as the Republican Party grew in influence. In 1978 Thad Cochran was elected to the United States Senate, the first Republican to hold that office in Mississippi since the Reconstruction. The Republican Party continued gaining ground in the state legislature, and in 1992 the state elected its first Republican governor. During the last decades of the twentieth century the traditional "good ole boy" political network also began to change. More women were elected to the legislature, and in 1976 Evelyn Gandy became the state's first female lieutenant governor. Six years later Lenore Prather was appointed as Mississippi's first female Supreme Court justice. By the turn of the twenty-first century the state legislature included a number of women, along with dozens of African Americans.

What has emerged in the modern era is a New Mississippi, a state that defies traditional regional stereotypes. While racial problems have not completely disappeared, today whites and blacks live side by side, coexisting in harmony with one another. The state's past is just that, and most Mississippians prefer to concentrate on the future. Industry and technology are vital components of Mississippi's economy, as is scientific agriculture. Students excel in Mississippi's public schools, community colleges, private colleges, and state universities. Health care in Mississippi has improved dramatically over the last half-

Catfish Capital of the World

During the 1960s catfish was introduced to Mississippi as a new cash crop and catfish farming soon became one of the state's most important industries. Today there are approximately 150,000 acres of catfish ponds in the United States and more than half (91,000) are in Mississippi. The state's ponds produce 75% of the nation's catfish and generate more than a quarter of a billion dollars annually. In 1976 catfish farming was having such an impact on Humphreys County that civic leaders there organized a festival to celebrate the industry. The first World Catfish Festival was held that year on the courthouse square in Belzoni, the county seat. About 3,000 people attended the event, which was held as part of the county's bicentennial celebration. Since then the festival has grown into one of Mississippi's major annual events. The World Catfish Festival in Belzoni draws 20,000 or more who enjoy a wide range of entertainment and take part in various activities. Little wonder that Humphreys County proudly bills itself as the "Catfish Capital of the World."

century, with the University of Mississippi Medical Center in Jackson leading the way. Thousands of tourists visit the state each year to take advantage of Mississippi's natural resources, hunting and fishing in the state's fields, streams, and forests. Others come to experience the Old South and the New South in the state's museums and art galleries. Some flock to the state in large numbers to roll dice, play cards, spin the roulette wheel, or challenge the "one-armed bandits" in the state's casinos. Today, few negative vestiges of the "old" Mississippi remain as the last half-century has seen dramatic change. Mississippians have not forgotten the negative elements of their collective past, but in most circles they have forgiven it.

Casino Gambling

In 1990 the state legislature passed the Mississippi Gaming Control Act, making Mississippi the third state to legalize dockside gambling. The law restricted casinos to coastal waters and the Mississippi River, and the state's first casino opened in 1992. The industry exploded in the so-called heart of the Bible Belt, and by 1995 Mississippi was the second largest gaming jurisdiction in the United States in terms of casino square footage, and third largest in gross revenues. Today, gaming is legal in nine of Mississippi's eighty-two counties and the industry employs over 38,000 people. Mississippi annually attracts more than 50 million casino visitors who wager more than $30 billion.

Hurricane Katrina

Members of the generation of Mississippians on the Gulf Coast who survived Hurricane Camille in 1969 never imagined that they would see another storm of such force. For decades Camille was the benchmark for hurricanes—that is, until August of 2005 when Hurricane Katrina blew ashore with devastating consequences. Wreaking havoc along the coastline from Mobile to New Orleans, Katrina

Hurricane Katrina damage on the Mississippi coast.
Agency: Dreamstime.com

destroyed much of the Mississippi Gulf Coast. The storm completely washed away hundreds of waterfront homes and businesses and severely flooded thousands of inland structures. In the span of a few hours, thousands of Gulf Coast residents lost everything they owned and almost a million Mississippians were left for days without electricity. "Katrina completely devastated our entire coastline,"

Mississippi governor Haley Barbour reported soon after surveying the damage. "The miles upon miles of utter destruction is unimaginable." The storm killed more than two hundred Mississippians and financial losses were in the billions. In the storm's immediate aftermath unemployment in the state's coastal counties skyrocketed, as did reports of sanitation problems and disease. The initial cleanup effort took months to complete and the overall recovery process will be measured in terms of years. Despite the hardships, resilient Mississippians along the Gulf Coast are determined to bring the area back as quickly as possible, and plans are already going forward to do just that. One state official summed up the prevailing point in the area shortly after the disaster when he told a crowd "We will rebuild the Coast and south Mississippi bigger and better than ever."

9

MISSISSIPPI'S CULTURAL HERITAGE

Throughout its history Mississippi has seen hard times. During the antebellum period much of the state was a wilderness. Even after a significant number of settlers moved into the region, traditional subsistence agriculture, which was subject to the whims of nature, left many whites struggling to make ends meet. Slaves struggled even harder, facing row after row of cotton each day in the shadow of wealthy planters' mansions. The Civil War was catastrophic. It killed and maimed thousands and destroyed the state's economy. After the war, white Mississippians struggled to make sense of the carnage, while black Mississippians struggled to make a place for themselves in a society that had been turned upside-down. For a century after the war both races struggled to cope. Plantations, poverty, and racial anxiety are part of Mississippi's complex history, which in turn gives Mississippians a unique cultural heritage. For generations black and white culture overlapped in a state where the races were supposed to be officially segregated. The resulting tension, and the environment that tension created, manifested itself literally in song and story, giving the state a cultural identity unlike any other. As a result, per capita Mississippi has produced more than its share of musicians, writers, and artists. Some struggled for years in anonymity while others became nationally known. Here are just a few:

MUSICIANS AND SINGERS

Mose Allison (1927–)
Known as "The William Faulkner of Jazz," Mose Allison was born in Tippo, a small Delta town about twenty-five miles north of Greenwood. He grew up playing piano in the back of a local gas station and later attended the University of Mississippi and Louisiana State University,

where he studied philosophy and literature. After a stint in the army he moved to New York where he honed his skills as a blues and jazz pianist. In 1956 he released his first album on Prestige Records and later recorded for Columbia Records and Atlantic Records. Allison's blending of jazz and blues, along with his songwriting, earned him a reputation among fellow musicians and fans alike as one of popular music's great innovators. Though now in his seventies, he continues to tour.

Bo Diddley (1928–)

Born in McComb as Ellas Bates, Bo Diddley is widely hailed as a musical pioneer whose unique rhythmic style helped create a bridge between traditional blues and rock-and-roll. A frustrated drummer, Diddley studied violin for twelve years, and his sister gave him his first guitar in 1940. He moved to Chicago with his family, and there during the 1950s he began playing with a local group in juke joints and on street corners. In 1955 he convinced Leonard and Phil Chess of Chess Records to record him and immediately produced a double A-side disc, *Bo Diddley/I'm A Man*, which went straight to the top of the rhythm and blues charts and established him as a major star. He recorded a number of other tracks with Chess over the next several years and was a major influence on many of the British groups that would conquer America during the 1960s. In commenting on his truly original sound, Diddley once said simply "I play the guitar as if I'm playing drums....I play drum licks on the guitar."

Faith Hill (1967–)

One of the most successful country music and crossover artists of all time, Faith Hill fittingly grew up in the town of Star, about fifteen miles south of Jackson. She started singing at family gatherings at age three, and by age seventeen she was performing at local rodeos. Following her dream of becoming a professional singer, she moved to Nashville where her initial attempts at breaking into the music business failed. Hill eventually found a job singing backup for songwriter–musician Gary Burr and later came to the attention of Warner Brothers Records. Her first single, "Wild One," topped the country charts in 1994,

Delta Blues Museum

Located in Clarksdale, the cradle of the blues, the Delta Blues Museum pays tribute to a musical genre that is at once both sad and celebratory. The museum is housed in a former railroad depot that was built in 1918. It includes more than 11,000 square feet of exhibits. Visitors from all over the world come to Clarksdale each year to learn about the blues and about the artists who have produced the music. The museum's collection includes photographs, instruments, recordings, and other artifacts related to blues greats such as Muddy Waters, Howlin' Wolf, Elmore James, John Lee Hooker, and of course Robert Johnson, who supposedly sold his soul to the Devil at a nearby crossroads in exchange for musical talent. Clarksdale also includes a number of other blues-related landmarks, as well as clubs where visitors can celebrate the blues first hand.

beginning an amazing string of hit singles and albums that earned her multiple Grammy awards and almost every award available in the country music industry. She has performed at many high profile events, including the Super Bowl and the Olympics, and her image has graced the covers of countless national magazines. Today, Hill continues to tour and record, working on solo projects and in collaboration with her husband, country music artist Tim McGraw.

John Lee Hooker (1917–2001)

One of the most prolific blues artists in history, John Lee Hooker was born in Vance, about thirty miles south of Clarksdale. He learned the guitar from his stepfather and was already a seasoned performer in 1943 when he moved to Detroit, where he worked days as a janitor and nights playing in local clubs. He began his recording career in 1948 with "Boogie Chillen" and "Wednesday Evening Blues," which quickly became hits in the African-American community. Over the next five decades he recorded more than five hundred songs and dozens of albums, eventually becoming popular among whites during the blues revival of the 1960s. Until his death in 2001 he played or recorded with many of the major acts of the rock era, who hailed him as a founding father of the genre.

Elmore James (1910–1963)

Born on a small plantation in Canton, Elmore James became one of the great apostles of modern blues music. Forsaking farm labor, he lived his adult life as an itinerate musician, touring the South with a number of blues artists including Robert Jr. Lockwood, son of the legendary Robert Johnson. James was influenced by Johnson and others, but his originality sprang from his furious use of the bottleneck when playing guitar. In 1952 he scored a major hit with a remake of Johnson's "Dust My Broom." He also wrote a number of blues standards, most notably "The Sky is Crying" and "Everyday I Have the Blues," songs that would be covered again and again by other artists. Like many southern bluesmen, James first gained acclaim in England before being "discovered" by white American audiences during the blues revival of the 1960s. Unfortunately he would not live to see blues music, and particularly his music, gain widespread acceptance. James died in 1963, just before the so-called British Invasion brought blues music to the white masses in the United States.

Robert Johnson (1912–1938)

Blues music's most legendary character, Robert Johnson was born in Hazelhurst but spent much of his life traveling from place to place, supporting himself by playing guitar and singing at parties and in juke joints. As the story goes, Johnson sold his soul to the Devil at a Delta crossroads in exchange for extraordinary musical talent. While in Texas in 1936 and 1937 he recorded twenty-nine songs that would prove to be his legacy. His original compositions, including "Dust My Broom," "Crossroads," "Sweet Home Chicago," and "Love in Vain," have been covered by generations of blues and rock artists. Drinking and carousing were the inspiration for some of his work, and eventually became his downfall. While still in his twenties, Johnson died after supposedly being poisoned in a juke joint by a jealous husband.

B. B. King (1925–)
Born near Indianola in the Mississippi Delta, bluesman B. B.
King received his first guitar from a relative at the age of
nine. As a kid he sang in church and later worked as a disc
jockey in Greenville. After World War II, King moved to
Memphis, where he began his career as a professional
musician. He was one of the first blues artists to record in the
city, and through radio station WDIA "Blues Boy" B. B.
King became well known in the region. He moved to Los
Angeles in the early 1950s, where he produced hit after hit
including "Everyday," "Sweet Little Angel," and "Three
O'clock Blues." In 1969 he released one of his biggest
commercial records, *The Thrill is Gone*. One of the most
popular and high-profile blues artists ever, King has
performed all over the world, earning the title "Ambassador
of the Blues."

Elvis Presley (1935–1977)
Arguably the world's most famous entertainer, and
certainly the world's most famous Mississippian, Elvis
Presley was born in a two-room shack in Tupelo. His
family later moved to Memphis, where in 1954 he made his
first recording for Sam Phillips's Sun Records. That year
Presley became a regional star with the release of "That's
Alright Mama," and a national celebrity in 1956 with the
release of "Heartbreak Hotel" on the RCA label. Over the
next two decades Presley sold millions of records, made
countless television appearances, and starred in more than
thirty films. He was proclaimed "The King" of rock-and-
roll, and every rock performer that followed him felt his
influence. By the 1970s Presley had become a major figure
in American popular culture and an international star. His
untimely death in 1977 at the age of 42 shocked the world
and deified him in the minds of many. Since it was opened
to the public in 1982, Graceland, Presley's Memphis home,
has become a major tourist attraction visited by millions
from around the globe.

Leontyne Price (1927–)
Born in Laurel, Mary Violet Leontyne Price displayed her
talents at an early age. Her formal music instruction began
with piano lessons at age five, and she grew up using her

extraordinary voice as part of her church choir. After graduating from Oak Park High School in 1944 and earning a B.A. at Wilberforce (Ohio) College in 1948, she attended Juilliard School of Music in New York on a full tuition scholarship. While attending Juilliard she appeared in a revival of Gershwin's *Porgy and Bess*, which toured the United States and Europe. In 1955 an appearance on the National Broadcasting Company's Opera Theater marked her professional debut in grand opera, and her first appearance in a major opera house took place two years later in San Francisco. On January 27, 1961 Price made her Metropolitan Opera debut as Leonora in Verdi's *Il Trovatore* and later that year became the first African American to open a Metropolitan Opera season. These performances generated rave reviews and established her as a major star. Her reputation grew through the 1960s and 1970s as she played to packed houses and made recordings that earned her eighteen Grammy awards. Price also appeared on the cover of *Time*, was awarded the Presidential Freedom Award, and received numerous international accolades recognizing her talent. She retired after a final performance on January 3, 1985.

Elvis Presley Birthplace

Tupelo's most significant tourist attraction, and one of the city's most important buildings, is the simple two-room house where Elvis Presley was born on January 8, 1935. The Elvis Presley birthplace is part of Elvis Presley Park and has been restored to the period when the singer's family lived there. Presley's father Vernon built the house at a total cost of $180, and Elvis occasionally came back to visit the modest home after he achieved international fame. In addition to the house, the park includes the Elvis Presley Museum, Memorial Chapel, and recreation facilities for picnics and community events. The museum houses a unique collection of articles from the rock-and-roll icon's early life and career. Thousands visit the site each year, particularly around the anniversaries of Presley's birth and death.

Charley Pride (1938–)

One of eleven children born to a sharecropper in the Delta town of Sledge, Charlie Pride used his musical talents to reach the pinnacle of success in the country music industry. In the process he became a pioneer as the first African-American country artist to enter the mainstream. Pride's dream of becoming a professional baseball player actually helped lead to his music career. He struggled in the minor leagues for several years, singing and playing his guitar during his off hours for his teammates and informally in local venues as he crossed the country. His baseball career ended, but a local night club performance caught the attention of Red Sovine, which led to an audition in Nashville for Chet Atkins and eventually a contract with RCA. Pride released his first single, "The Snakes Crawl at Night," in 1966, but his race was kept secret during the release of his first three singles. While Pride met some resistance when his race became public, his music carried the day and he gained widespread acceptance. He was named Entertainer of the Year by the Country Music Association in 1971 and was named the association's Male Vocalist of the Year in 1971 and 1972, the first artist to win that award in consecutive years. In 1993 Pride was inducted into the Grand Ole Opry, and he was elected to the Country Music Hall of Fame in 2000. He has recorded twenty-nine number one singles, including his signature songs "Is Anybody Goin' to San Antone" and "Kiss an Angel Good Morning."

Jimmie Rodgers (1897–1933)

Known affectionately in Nashville as "The Man Who Started It All," country music trailblazer James Charles Rodgers was born the son of a railroad worker near Meridian. As a young man he worked on the railroad but was plagued by poor health. Diagnosed with tuberculosis early in life, he retired from the railroad and turned to his first love, music, to make a living. Rodgers traveled throughout the South performing at country fairs, in honkytonks, and on street corners. Answering a newspaper advertisement, he auditioned for Ralph Peer, a record producer for the Victor Talking Machine Company. Peer recognized Rodgers's talent and first recorded him in August of 1927. Rodgers eventually recorded over one hundred songs and in the process became country music's first bona fide star. His original compositions, including "Sleep Baby Sleep," "Blue Yodel #9," and "My Rough and Rowdy Ways," became country standards. Tragically, Rodgers's recording career lasted only six years. He succumbed to tuberculosis in New York City on May 26, 1933, less than two days after making his last record. His death was mourned by millions, and his influence would be felt by every country music performer to follow him. When the Country Music Hall of Fame was established in 1961, Jimmie Rodgers was the first person inducted.

The Jimmie Rodgers Museum

During the late 1920s it was said that the most popular request in general stores throughout the South was for "a dozen eggs, a pound of butter, and the latest Jimmie Rodgers record." Rodgers is acknowledged as the Father of Country Music and his success as an early recording star helped create the country music industry. The Jimmie Rodgers Museum is located in Meridian, Rogers's hometown, and houses a variety of artifacts related to the singer and the early years of country music. One of the centerpieces of the collection is Rodgers's custom-made 1928 Martin guitar. In addition to the museum, Meridian hosts an annual Jimmie Rodgers Festival to celebrate the life of its most famous son. Thousands attend the festival each year, and entertainment for the event is provided by some of country music's most prominent stars.

Howlin' Wolf (1910–1976)

Born Chester Arthur Burnett near West Point, bluesman Howlin' Wolf possessed one of the most powerful and distinct voices ever recorded. Though he was never completely proficient on the guitar, and could barely count to keep formal time, he gained worldwide fame as a blues pioneer whose gruff, gravely sound made a lasting impression on all who heard it. Wolf's early life was marked by poverty. In 1923 he moved with his family to

Clarksdale, Mississippi, where he worked on a large plantation for years. He moved to Memphis after World War II and found work as a disc jockey while also leading his own band at night. His radio show allowed him to acquire a significant following around the South, as did recordings he made for noted producer Sam Phillips in 1948. He eventually moved to Chicago after signing an exclusive contract to record with Chess Records, and he remained there for the rest of his life. Among his classic recordings for Chess were "The Red Rooster," "Whose Been Talking," and "Spoonful." The Rolling Stones introduced him to the British public in 1964 and he benefited from the so-called British Invasion of rock groups, many of whom acknowledged him an influence. Wolf continued making records until his death in 1976.

Muddy Waters (1915–1983)

Born McKinley Morganfield near Rolling Fork, Muddy Waters went on to become a central figure in the history of blues music as one of the creators of the electric "Chicago" blues style. As a young man Waters drove a tractor on a cotton plantation during the day and played music at night in local clubs. He left the South in 1943 bound for Chicago, where his unique talent soon gained him a following in the city's black night clubs. Always the innovator, he used an electric guitar and bottleneck to produce a gritty sound that came to the attention of Leonard and Marshall Chess of Chess Records. Waters made a number of records for Chess and put together a band that included many of the greatest blues artists of the period. His songs, such as "Rolling Stone," "Honey Bee," "Baby Please Don't Go," and "I'm Ready," became instant standards. Waters gained international acclaim during the 1960s when British rock groups like the Rolling Stones, who took their name from the Waters song, exposed the American masses to blues music. As a result, he achieved his greatest commercial success during the latter years of his life. Hailed as the "father of the blues," Waters continued to tour America and Europe until his death in 1983.

Authors

William Faulkner (1897–1962)

Born in New Albany, William Faulkner is one of Mississippi's most famous sons. He grew up in Oxford, where his father was employed for several years at the University of Mississippi, and he drew on his small-town Southern upbringing as inspiration for much of his finest work. Most of Faulkner's novels and short stories are set in the fictional town of Jefferson, seat of government for equally fictional Yoknapatawpha County. They deal with some of the deepest themes of the human existence: love and hate, class and race, honor, jealousy, and greed. Among his most famous works are *The Sound and the Fury* (1929), *Absalom, Absalom* (1936), *Intruder in the Dust* (1947), and *The Reivers* (1962). Faulkner gained great acclaim during his lifetime and was rewarded for his talents with both the Pulitzer and Nobel Prizes. His writings have been translated into many languages and his books are popular throughout the world. Faulkner died in 1962 and was buried in Oxford, where his grave is still a frequent stop for tourists.

Rowan Oak

By 1930 William Faulkner had sold enough stories to allow him to buy an antebellum home in Oxford. He purchased what was known as the old Shegog place, a two-story Greek Revival house built about 1844, with grounds that included a smokehouse and barn. At the time he purchased the home it had fallen into disrepair, with sagging beams and no electricity or plumbing. Doing much of the work himself, Faulkner renovated the house and, in so doing, created a sanctuary where he would produce some of his most famous works. He named his home Rowan Oak, after the legend of the Rowan tree, which the Celts believed offered protection and safety. Since 1972 the University of Mississippi has administered the home and today Rowan Oak is open to the public. It remains much as Faulkner left it, with his black manual typewriter on display along with an outline of his Pulitzer Prizewinning novel *A Fable* scrawled on one of the walls in the author's hand.

Margaret Walker Alexander (1915–1998)

The daughter of a minister and a teacher, Margaret Walker was born in 1915 in Birmingham, Alabama. She was encouraged by her parents to excel and as a child read a great deal of poetry and philosophy. In 1935 she graduated from Northwestern in Chicago with a degree in English and the following year joined the Federal Writer's Project, where she worked with other prominent writers including Richard Wright, Frank Yerby, and Gwendolyn Brooks. In 1942 Walker earned a master's degree in creative writing from the University of Iowa, and later earned a PhD in English from the university. She won the Yale Younger Poets Competition for her volume of poetry titled *For My People*. After her marriage to Firnist James Alexander, Walker taught at Livingston College in North Carolina and at West Virginia State College before moving to Mississippi in 1949 to accept an English professorship at Jackson State College. In 1966 she completed her landmark novel *Jubilee*, which won the Houghton Mifflin Literary Fellowship Award and sparked renewed public interest in her work. In 1970 she produced *Prophets for a New Day* and, three years later, *October Journey*. Walker taught at Jackson State until 1979, after which she toured, lectured, and continued to write. She made her home in Jackson until her death in 1998.

Hodding Carter (1907–1972)

Born in Louisiana, Hodding Carter made a name for himself as a crusading author and newspaperman in Greenville, Mississippi. Carter was educated at Bowdoin College in Maine and at Columbia University, where he studied journalism. In 1929 he joined the staff of the New Orleans *Item-Tribune* and later became night manager for United Press in New Orleans. During the early 1930s Carter moved to Hammond, Louisiana, where he launched the *Daily Courier* newspaper and began writing political editorials critical of Louisiana's Senator Huey Long. He later moved to Greenville and established the *Delta Democrat Times*. After World War II he began writing editorials against racial intolerance, which resulted in his being awarded the Pulitzer Prize. In addition to his newspaper work, Carter wrote articles for a number of national publications and produced several books, including *Southern Legacy* (1950), *Where Main Street Meets the River* (1953), and *The Angry Scar* (1959). A few years before his death in 1972, he relinquished the editorship of his newspaper to his son, Hodding Carter III, who became well known as a State Department spokesman for President Jimmy Carter's administration.

Shelby Foote (1916–2005)

The only child of a union between two old Delta families, Shelby Dade Foote, Jr. was born in Greenville in 1916. For most of the next thirty-five years he lived in the Delta town, and many of his best works explored the intricacies and contradictions of the Southern existence. Foote attended the University of North Carolina for a time before returning home and getting a job writing for a local newspaper. He served in World War II and afterwards produced several stories that were accepted for publication in the *Saturday Evening Post*. His first novel, *Tournament*, was published in 1949, followed by *Follow Me Down* (1950), *Love in a Dry Season* (1951), and *Shiloh* (1952). Foote's early work earned him a solid reputation in literary circles. In 1954 he moved to Memphis, where he began a massive three-volume work, *The Civil War: A Narrative*, which would take twenty years to complete. Though well-respected, Foote toiled in relative obscurity until his 1990 appearance in Ken Burns's *The Civil War*, a widely watched and critically acclaimed PBS documentary. Foote's segments in the program capitalized on his unique talents as a storyteller, and the documentary transformed him into a national celebrity. Sales of his books increased, he appeared on NBC's *Tonight Show*, and articles about him appeared in *Newsweek,* the *New York Times*, and the *Washington Post*. After all of the publicity surrounding the program, Foote was in demand for interviews and on the speaking circuit.

John Grisham (1955–)

Mississippi's most widely sold author, John Grisham, was born in Jonesboro, Arkansas in 1955 and moved to Southaven in 1967. He graduated from Mississippi State University in 1977 and received a law degree from the

University of Mississippi four years later. Grisham established a law practice and in 1983 was elected to the state legislature. He published his first novel, *A Time to Kill*, in 1989. It sold modestly and received some good reviews. His next book, *The Firm,* established the author's international reputation. In 1990, before the novel was published, Paramount Pictures bought the film rights to *The Firm* and produced the popular film starring Tom Cruise. Since then Grisham has become one of the world's best-selling novelists, producing a string of works including *The Pelican Brief, The Client, The Chamber*, and *The Rainmaker*, all of which were turned into successful films. Grisham continues to write extremely popular books and divides his time between homes in Oxford and Charlottesville, Virginia.

Willie Morris (1934–1999)

A sixth generation Mississippian, Willie Morris was born in 1934 in Jackson and moved with his family to Yazoo City before his first birthday. After graduating from high school he attended the University of Texas and, as a senior, became editor of the school's newspaper. As editor, he incurred the wrath of the Board of Regents for his scathing attacks on segregation, censorship, and the state's oil and gas interests. He graduated as a Rhodes Scholar and earned B.A. and M.A. degrees at New College, Oxford University. In 1963 he was hired at *Harper's Magazine*, where he became editor-in-chief in 1967. As editor Morris attracted contributions from some of America's premier writers and dramatically enhanced the magazine's reputation. In 1980 Morris returned to Mississippi, where he became writer in residence at the University of Mississippi. Like many Southern authors, Morris spent a lifetime trying to explain the complexities of the Southern existence to the outside world. Among his most notable works are *North Toward Home, My Dog Skip, Good Old Boy, The Last of the Southern Girls, The Ghost of Medgar Evers*, and *New York Days*. When Morris died in 1999 national commentators sang his praises and lengthy obituaries celebrated his achievements. He was buried in Yazoo City.

Eudora Welty (1909–2001)

Born in 1909 in Jackson, Eudora Welty was a life-long resident of Mississippi's capital city. The product of a comfortable middle-class home, she attended Mississippi University for Women and later graduated from the University of Wisconsin. She then earned a business degree from Columbia University in New York City, quite a feat for a female in 1931. She returned to Jackson during the Great Depression and worked as a publicist for the Works Progress Administration. In that capacity she toured Mississippi taking photographs, talking to people, and as it turned out, collecting images and inspiration for her first collection of stories, *A Curtain of Green*, published in 1941. For the rest of her life Welty wrote about Mississippi and the Southern experience, earning a Pulitzer Prize and many other accolades for her efforts. Among her many notable works are *The Robber Bridegroom, The Ponder Heart, Losing Battles*, and *Delta Wedding*. While the events she describes in her books are local, the themes that she explores—isolation, humor, tragedy, and triumph—are universal, and her writing has been translated into many languages and read around the world. All of Mississippi mourned her death and celebrated her long and fruitful life on July 23, 2001.

Tennessee Williams (1911–1983)

One of America's greatest playwrights, Tennessee Williams was born in Columbus in 1911. His family lived for several years in Clarksdale before moving to St. Louis in 1918. There, at the age of sixteen, Williams achieved his first literary success, winning a five-dollar third prize for an essay. He attended the University of Missouri and in 1931 began working for the St. Louis Shoe Company. His first play was produced in 1937, but he did not gain national acclaim until 1944 when what many consider to be his finest work, *The Glass Menagerie*, had a successful run in Chicago and subsequently took Broadway by storm. A string of incredible successes followed as Williams's plays *A Streetcar Named Desire* (for which he won a Pulitzer Prize), *Summer and Smoke, A Rose Tattoo*, and *Camino Real* thrust him into the upper echelons of New York's literary and theatrical circles. He won a second

Pulitzer Prize in 1955 for *Cat on a Hot Tin Roof* and gained even more acclaim as his works were turned into successful motion pictures. Most of Williams's plays were set in the South and communicated unique and powerful insights into Southern life. After *Night of the Iguana* (1962) his plays failed to achieve the widespread popularity of his earlier work, but Williams continued to write and be produced. He died in New York City in 1983 and was buried in St. Louis.

Richard Wright (1908–1960)

One of America's finest authors, Richard Wright was also one of the first African-American writers to achieve widespread literary fame. Wright was born in 1908 near Natchez, the son of an illiterate sharecropper and an educated school teacher. After his father abandoned the family, Wright moved with his mother to Arkansas, Tennessee, and back to Mississippi. He spent his early life in poverty, working at menial jobs in the segregated South. In hopes of escaping the racism and limited opportunities that his region afforded African Americans, Wright moved to Chicago and then to New York, where he found employment with the Federal Writer's Project. His first novel, *Uncle Tom's Children*, was published in 1938, and the next year he received a Guggenheim Fellowship that allowed him to write *Native Son* (1940). The latter work was a great success and was translated into six languages. In 1945 Wright published an autobiographical novel, *Black Boy*, which further established his reputation in the literary world. The central theme of Wright's early work was the struggle of an African-American male against racial prejudice and the social environment that it spawned. Realizing that discrimination was not limited to the South, Wright became angry and disenchanted with the United States and subsequently moved to France in 1946. A year later he became a French citizen. Wright remained overseas for the rest of his life, dying in Paris in 1960.

Walter Anderson Museum of Art

Located in historic Ocean Springs on the Gulf Coast, the Walter Anderson Museum of Art (WAMA) opened in 1991 to celebrate the legacy of Walter Inglis Anderson (1903–1965), one of America's unique artistic talents. The museum houses on permanent display many of Anderson's watercolors, drawings, oils, and block prints, along with pieces by Anderson's two brothers, Peter Anderson (1901–1984) and James McConnell Anderson (1907–1998), talented artists in their own right. Many of Walter Anderson's works depict the plants, animals, and people of the Mississippi Gulf Coast. Throughout the year the museum also includes diverse rotating exhibits as well as the works of other artists.

OTHER PERSONALITIES WITH MISSISSIPPI CONNECTIONS

Musicians/Singers
Jimmy Buffett
Moe Bandy
W. C. Handy
Brandi Norwood
Charley Patton
LeAnn Rimes
Marty Stuart
Ike Turner
Conway Twitty
Tammy Wynette

The Arts
Walter Anderson, artist
Stephen Ambrose, writer
Sherwood Bonner, writer
John Butler, choreographer
Ellen Douglas, writer
Ellen Gilchrist, novelist
Beth Henley, playwright

Walker Percy, novelist
James Street, novelist
Zig Zigler, speaker, writer

Entertainers
Dana Andrews, actor
Jerry Clower, comedian
John Dye, actor
Morgan Freeman, actor
Jim Henson, creator of the Muppets
James Earl Jones, actor
Dianne Ladd, actor
Gerald McRaney, actor
Bob Pittman, founder of MTV
Eric Roberts, actor
Sela Ward, actor
Oprah Winfrey, actor/talk show host

Chronology of Major Events

c. 10,000 BCE Small bands of nomadic humans first reach the area that would become the state of Mississippi.

8000 BCE–1800 BCE Archaic Period, during which native cultures in Mississippi become better defined and more regionalized.

1800 BCE–1000 CE Woodland Period, during which ceremonial mound building among the native cultures is introduced.

1000–1700 CE Mississippian Period, during which there is a resurgence of mound building among the native cultures. Choctaws, Chickasaws, and Natchez emerge as Mississippi's most powerful tribes.

1540–41 Hernando de Soto, Spanish explorer, becomes the first-known European to enter Mississippi. Credited with "discovering" the Mississippi River.

1673 Fur trapper Louis Joliet and French missionary Jacques Marquette begin exploration of the Mississippi River. They move south to the mouth of the Arkansas River, near present-day Rosedale, Mississippi, before turning back.

1682 Robert Cavalier de La Salle navigates the Mississippi River to its mouth and claims for France all lands drained by the river.

1699 Pierre LeMoyne, Sieur d'Iberville, and his brother Jean Baptiste, Sieur d'Bienville, land in what is now Ocean Springs, Mississippi. They build Fort Maurepas, the first permanent European settlement in Mississippi.

1716 The French establish Fort Rosalie on the site of present-day Natchez, Mississippi.

1729 The Natchez Indians massacre French settlers at Fort Rosalie in an effort to drive the Europeans from the area.

1731 The French retaliate for the massacre at Fort Rosalie by destroying the Natchez tribe.

1736 The Chickasaws defeat the French and their Choctaw allies at the Battle of Ackia, at present-day Tupelo, Mississippi.

1756–63 French and Indian War.

1763 The French and Indian War ends. West Florida, which includes part of Mississippi, comes under British control, as do other former French holdings east of the Mississippi River.

1775–83 American Revolution.

1779 The Spanish capture Natchez.

1783   Following the Treaty of Paris, West Florida comes under Spanish control, though the United States also lays claim to the region.

1795   Spain yields to the United States all land in Mississippi north of the 31st parallel, including Natchez.

1798   The United States organizes the Mississippi Territory. Winthrop Sargent becomes the territory's first governor.

1801   The Choctaws cede the Natchez District to the United States through the Treaty of Fort Adams. Thomas Jefferson appoints William C. C. Claiborne as Mississippi territorial governor.

1801–02 The Natchez Trace begins to develop as a mail route and major road. Mississippi moves its territorial capital from Natchez to Washington.

1803   The Louisiana Purchase increases commerce on the Mississippi River.

1805   The Choctaws cede 4.5 million acres of land to the United States through the Treaty of Mount Dexter. The land cession includes the state's Piney Woods region.

1810–13 Spain relinquishes its remaining claims in the Mississippi Territory.

1811   Jefferson College opens in Washington.

1812–15 The War of 1812.

1816   The Chickasaws cede a small portion of their holdings around the Tombigbee River in northern Mississippi to the United States through the Treaty of Fort Stephens.

1817   On December 10 Mississippi enters the Union as the twentieth state. David Holmes becomes the state's first governor.

1818   Elizabeth Female Academy is founded in Washington.

1820   The Choctaws cede five million more acres to the United States through the Treaty of Doak's Stand.

1821   Franklin Academy, Mississippi's first public school, opens in Columbus.

1822   Jackson becomes Mississippi's capital.

1826   Hampstead Academy, now Mississippi College, opens in Clinton.

1830   Choctaw removal begins through the Treaty of Dancing Rabbit Creek, which cedes the tribe's remaining land in Mississippi to the United States. Most of the Choctaws relocate to the Indian Territory (present-day Oklahoma) west of the Mississippi River.

1832   The Chickasaws give up their remaining lands in Mississippi through the Treaty of Pontotoc. Mississippi produces its second constitution.

1839   Official business is conducted for the first time in

Mississippi's new state capitol building.

1842   Governor Tilghman M. Tucker becomes the state's first chief executive to occupy the newly completed Governor's Mansion.

1844   The University of Mississippi is established at Oxford.

1846–48 The Mexican War. Many Mississippians participate in the war effort and Jefferson Davis gains fame as a military hero.

1848   The state government assumes operation of a private school for the blind, which becomes the Mississippi School for the Blind, the nation's first state-supported institution for the handicapped.

1850   Much of the Mississippi Delta is drained, cleared, and for the first time becomes available for cultivation. The United States' "first secession crisis" ends with the Compromise of 1850.

1851   Unionist Henry Foote defeats Jefferson Davis for governor.

1854   Henry Hughes of Port Gibson publishes *Treatise on Sociology*, which later earns him the title "first American sociologist." The Kansas–Nebraska Act dramatically increases tension between the slaveholding and non-slaveholding states.

1857   The Dred Scott decision further inflames tensions between the North and the South over slavery.

1861   Mississippi secedes from the Union on January 9. In July, Union forces capture Ship Island, giving the Union control of the Mississippi Gulf Coast. Jefferson Davis becomes president of the Confederate States of America.

1862   Corinth, Mississippi, a vital Southern railroad center, falls to the Union a few weeks after the Battle of Shiloh.

1863   Abraham Lincoln issues the Emancipation Proclamation. Jackson and Vicksburg surrender to Federal forces.

1864   Nathan Bedford Forrest achieves a major victory at the Battle of Brice's Crossroads in northeastern Mississippi.

1865   The Civil War ends. Abraham Lincoln is assassinated. Andrew Johnson appoints William L. Sharkey provisional governor of Mississippi. The Freedmen's Bureau is established.

1865–67 Confederate veteran Benjamin G. Humphreys is elected governor and the Mississippi Legislature passes Black Codes. Mississippi's initial attempt to re-enter the Union is rejected by Congress.

1866   Rust College is established in Holly Springs.

1867	A military government is established in Mississippi after the reconstructed government of Mississippi is rejected by Congress.
1868	Mississippi's first biracial constitutional convention—the so-called Black and Tan Convention—drafts a constitution protecting the rights of freedmen, former slaves.
1869	James L. Alcorn becomes governor and Republican rule officially begins in Mississippi.
1870	Mississippi is readmitted to the Union on February 23. The state's first system of public education is established. Hiram Revels, a minister from Natchez, becomes the first Africa-American senator in United States history.
1871	Alcorn Agricultural and Mechanical College, now Alcorn State University, is organized at Lorman.
1873	Adelbert Ames is elected governor.
1875	Through highly questionable means in many places, the Democratic Party regains control of Mississippi's government.
1877	The Mississippi State Board of Health is created.
1878	Mississippi Agricultural and Mechanical College, now Mississippi State University, is established at Starkville. Thousand are affected by a serious yellow fever epidemic.
1884	The Industrial Institute and College, now Mississippi University for Women, is established at Columbus.
1885–90	Mississippi begins enacting Jim Crow laws, legalizing segregation.
1890	Mississippi adopts a new state constitution designed to disenfranchise most African Americans.
1892	Millsaps College opens in Jackson.
1896	*Plessy v. Ferguson* upholds the South's Jim Crow laws.
1903	A new state capitol building opens in Jackson.
1907	The boll weevil arrives in Mississippi, destroying most of the state's cotton crop.
1908	Mississippi adopts statewide prohibition.
1909	Dr. Laurence C. Jones founds the Piney Woods Country Life School for African Americans.
1910	Mississippi Normal College, now the University of Southern Mississippi, is organized at Hattiesburg.
1914–18	World War I.
1922	The state legislature authorizes a system of junior colleges, the first in the nation.
1924	Delta State Teachers' College, now Delta State University, is established.

1927	The Mississippi River floods almost three million acres in the Delta. Thousands are left homeless.
1929	The Great Depression begins.
1932	The state's first sales tax becomes effective.
	The Natchez Pilgrimage, a tour of that area's antebellum homes, becomes an annual event.
1933	Nationally famous recording artist and Mississippian Jimmie Rodgers dies soon after his last recording session.
1936	During Governor Hugh White's administration, the state legislature passes an amendment to balance agriculture with industry (BAWI Program).
1941–45	World War II promotes an industrial boom in the state.
1946	Mississippi Vocational College, now Mississippi Valley State University, is established at Itta Bena.
1954	The landmark Supreme Court case *Brown vs. Board of Education* signals the beginning of the end of segregation in the South. Citizens' Council movement begins.
1956	State Sovereignty Commission is established to fight integration.
1962	James Meredith becomes the first African American to enroll at the University of Mississippi.
1963	NAACP Field Secretary Medgar Evers is murdered in Jackson.
1964	Freedom Summer. Andrew Goodman, Michael Schwerner, and James Chaney are murdered as a result of their civil rights work in Mississippi.
1965–70	More Mississippians begin working in industry than in agriculture.
1968	Robert Clark becomes the first African American since Reconstruction to serve in the Mississippi House of Representatives.
1969	Hurricane Camille severely damages the Mississippi Gulf Coast.
1970	Most of Mississippi's public schools are desegregated. Mississippi Authority for Educational Television is established and begins broadcasting.
1972	Work begins on the Tennessee-Tombigbee Waterway.
1978	Thad Cochran becomes the first Mississippi Republican elected to the United States Senate since Reconstruction.
1979	The Pearl River overflows its banks, causing a devastating flood in Jackson and other parts of the state.
1982	Governor William F. Winter calls a special legislative session, resulting in adoption of the historic Education Reform Act, a major step in the process of school

reform. Jackson hosts the International Ballet Competition.

1983   Judge Lenore Prather becomes Mississippi's first woman Supreme Court justice.

1984   Public Radio begins broadcasting in Mississippi.

1985   Reuben Anderson becomes Mississippi's first black Supreme Court justice.

1986   The Tennessee-Tombigbee Waterway is completed. Mike Espy becomes the first African American since Reconstruction elected to represent Mississippi in the United States House of Representatives.

1987   At age 39 Ray Mabus is elected the nation's youngest governor.

1990   Mississippi National Guard men and women play important roles in Operation Desert Storm in the Middle East. During a special session the Mississippi Legislature passed the Mississippi Gaming Control Act, paving the way for legalized gambling in the state.

1991   Mississippi becomes the nation's twenty-first state to allow its citizens to register to vote by mail. Kirk Fordice becomes Mississippi's first Republican governor since Reconstruction.

1992   Mississippi's first casino opens in Biloxi.

2005   Hurricane Katrina devastates the Mississippi Gulf Coast.

2006   The National Football League's New Orleans Saints agree to hold their annual summer training camp at Millsaps College in Jackson.

2007   In the most recent in a string of reopened civil rights cases, former Ku Klux Klansman James Ford Seale is convicted of the 1964 murders of African American teenagers Charles Eddie Moore and Henry Hezekiah Dee in Franklin County.

Historical Societies

1699 Historical Committee
PO Box 713
Ocean Springs, MS 39566-0713

Amite County Historical Society
PO Box 2
Liberty, MS 39645

Benton County Historical &
  Genealogical Society
PO Box 683
Ashland, MS 38603

Brice's Crossroads Visitors &
  Interpretive Center
607 Grisham Street
Baldwyn, MS 38824

Brookhaven Trust for the
  Preservation of History,
  Culture, & the Arts
PO Box 134
Brookhaven, MS 39602-0134

Calhoun County Historical &
  Genealogical Society
PO Box 114
Pittsboro, MS 38951

Chickasaw County Historical
  Society
PO Box 42
Houston, MS 38851

Columbus & Lowndes County
  Historical Society
124 4th Avenue South
Columbus, MS 39701

Dancing Rabbit Genealogical
  Society
PO Box 166
Carthage, MS 39051

Family Research Association
  of Mississippi, Inc.
PO Box 13334
Jackson, MS 39236-3334

Flora Area Historical Society
PO Box 356
Flora, MS 39071

Fort Maurepas Society
PO Box 1741
Ocean Springs, MS 39564-1741

Foundation for the
  Restoration of Boler's Inn
400 Bank Street
Union, MS 39365

Friars Point Historical
  Preservation Society
PO Box 95
Friars Point, MS 38631

Genealogical Society of
  DeSoto County
PO Box 607
Hernando, MS 38632-0607

Granly Danish Historical
  Foundation
6301 Country Lane
Pascagoula, MS 39581

Hattiesburg Area Historical
  Society
PO Box 1573
Hattiesburg, MS 39403-1573

Historic Clarke County, Inc.
PO Box 172
Quitman, MS 39355

Historic DeSoto Foundation
6920 East Center
Horn Lake, MS 38637

Historic Natchez Foundation
PO Box 1761
Natchez, MS 39121

Houlka Historical Society
1248 Hwy 15 N.
Houston, MS 38851

Itawamba Historical Society
PO Box 7
Mantachie, MS 38855

Jackson County 1699–1999
  Tricentennial Commission
6301 Country Lane
Pascagoula, MS 39581

Jackson County Genealogical
  Society
6301 Country Lane
Pascagoula, MS 39581

Jackson County Historical
  Society
4602 Fort Drive
Pascagoula, MS 39567

Kemper County Historical
  Association
PO Box 545
De Kalb, MS 39328-0545

Kosciusko-Attala Historical
  Society
PO Box 127
Kosciusko, MS 39090

Lauderdale County
  Department of Archives &
  History
PO Box 5511
Meridian, MS 39302-5511

Laurel-Jones County
  Historical Society
PO Box 4113
Laurel, MS 39441

Lawrence County Historical
  Society
PO Box 996
Monticello, MS 39654

Long Beach Historical Society
PO Box 244
Long Beach, MS 39560

Madison County Historical
  Society
535 East Center Street
Canton, MS 39046

Marion County Historical
  Society
One Hugh White Place
Columbia, MS 39429

Marshall County Historical
  Museum
PO Box 806
Holly Springs, MS 38635

Mississippi Coast Historical &
  Genealogical Society
PO Box 513
Biloxi, MS 39533-0513

Mississippi Cultural Crossroads
507 Market Street
Port Gibson, MS 39150

Mississippi Genealogical Society
PO Box 592
Calhoun City, MS 38916

Mississippi Junior Historical
  Society University of
  Southern Mississippi
Southern Station Box 5047
Hattiesburg, MS 39406-5047

Mississippi Vietnam Veterans
  Memorial Committee
PO Box 721
Biloxi, MS 39533-0721

Monroe County Historical
Society
PO Box 316
Aberdeen, MS 39730

Natchez Historical Society
PO Box 49
Natchez, MS 39121

Northeast Mississippi
Historical & Genealogical
Society
PO Box 434
Tupelo, MS 38802-0434

Noxubee County Historical
Society
PO Box 392
Macon, MS 39341

Oktibbeha County Historical
& Genealogical Society
PO Box 2290
Starkville, MS 39760

Olde Towne Clinton Historic
Preservation & Homeowners
Association
502 West College
Clinton, MS 39056

Oxford-Lafayette County
Heritage Foundation
PO Box 622
Oxford, MS 38655

Oxford Tourism Council
PO Box 965
Oxford, MS 38655
(662) 234-4680
(800) 758-9177
www.ci.oxford.ms.us
tourism@oxfordcenter.com

Panola County Historical &
Genealogical Society
788 Herron
Courtland, MS 38620

Panola Partnership, Inc.
150-A Public Square
Batesville, MS 38606
(662) 563-3126
(888) 872-6652
partnership@cableone.net

Pass Christian Historical Society
PO Box 58
Pass Christian, MS 39571

Pike County Historical Society
4327 Manhassett Drive
Jackson, MS 39211

Pontotoc County Historical
Society
PO Box 141
Pontotoc, MS 38863-0141

Preservation Society of
Ellicott Hill
215 South Pearl Street
Natchez, MS 39120

Rankin County Historical
Society
PO Box 841
Brandon, MS 39043

Simpson County Historical
Society
201 N. Congress
Mendenhall, MS 39114

Skipwith Historical &
Genealogical Society
PO Box 1382
Oxford, MS 38655

South Mississippi
Genealogical Society
PO Box 15271
Hattiesburg, MS 39404-5271

Sunflower County Historical
Society
c/o Sunflower County Library

201 Cypress Drive
Indianola, MS 38751

Tate County Genealogical &
  Historical Society
PO Box 974
Senatobia, MS 38668

Union County Historical Society
PO Box 657
New Albany, MS 38652

Vicksburg and Warren
  County Historical Society
1008 Cherry Street
Vicksburg, MS 39180

Vicksburg Foundation for
  Historic Preservation
PO Box 254
Vicksburg, MS 39181

Vicksburg Genealogical
  Society, Inc.
PO Box 1161
Vicksburg, MS 39181-1161

Walthall County Historical
  Society
700 Broad Street
Tylertown, MS 39667

Washington County
  Historical Society
166 Nowell Road
Greenville, MS 38703

Wayne County Genealogy
  Organization, Inc.
712 Wayne Street
Waynesboro, MS 39367

West Point/Clay County
  Cultural–Historical Arts
  Museum, Inc.
PO Box 1216
West Point, MS 39773

Woodville Civic Club, Inc.
PO Box 1055
Woodville, MS 39669

Yalobusha County Historical
  Society, Inc.
PO Box 258
Coffeeville, MS 38922

Yazoo Historical Society
  Triangle Cultural Center
PO Box 575
Yazoo City, MS 39194

State Parks

All of Mississippi's state parks are administered by:

Mississippi Department of Wildlife, Fisheries and Parks
PO Box 23093
Jackson, MS 39225-3093
1-800-GO-PARKS (1-800-467-2757)
or (601)304-2140

Buccaneer State Park
1150 South Beach Blvd.
Waveland, MS 39576
(228) 467-3822
(228) 467-2580 (wave pool)

Casey Jones Museum
10501 Vaughan Rd. #1
Vaughan, MS 39179
(601) 673-9864

Clarkco State Park
386 Clarkco Road
Quitman, MS 39355
(601) 776-6651

Florewood River Plantation
  and State Park
PO Box 680
Greenwood, MS 38930
(601) 455-3821

George Payne Cossar State Park
Route 1, Box 67
Oakland, MS 38948
(601) 623-7356

Golden Memorial State Park
Route 1, Box 8
Walnut Grove, MS 39189
(601) 253-2237

Great River Road State Park
PO Box 292
Rosedale, MS 38769
(601) 759-6762

Holmes County State Park
Route 1, Box 153
Durant, MS 39063
(601) 653-3351

Hugh White State Park
PO Box 725
Grenada, MS 38902-0725
(601) 226-4934

J. P. Coleman State Park
613 CR 321
Iuka, MS 38852
(601) 423-6515

John W. Kyle State Park
Route 1, Box 115
Sardis, MS 38666
(601) 487-1345

Lake Lowndes State Park
3319 Lake Lowndes Road
Columbus, MS 39702
(601) 328-2110

LeFleur's Bluff State Park and
  Golf Course
2140 Riverside Dr.
Jackson, MS 39202
(601) 987-3923
(601) 987-3998 (golf course)

Legion State Park
Route 5, Box 32-B
Louisville, MS 39339
(601) 773-8323

Leroy Percy State Park
PO Box 176
Hollandale, MS 38748
(601) 827-5436

Nanih Waiya Historic Site
Route 3, Box 251 A
Louisville, MS 39339
(60l) 773-7988

Natchez State Park
230-B Wickliff Rd.
Natchez, MS 39120
(610) 442-2658

Paul B. Johnson State Park
319 Geiger Lake Road
Hattiesburg, MS 39401
(60l) 582-7721

Percy Quin State Park
1156 Camp Beaver Drive
McComb, MS 39648
(601) 684-3938

Roosevelt State Park
2149 Hwy. 13 South
Morton, MS 39117
(601) 732-6316
(601) 732-6318 (food service)

Sam Dale Historic Site
PO Box 23093
Jackson, MS 39225-3093

Shepard State Park
1034 Graveline Road
Gautier, MS 39553
(228) 497-2244

Tishomingo State Park
PO Box 880
Tishomingo, MS 38873
(601) 438-6914

Tombigbee State Park
Route 2, Box 336 E
Tupelo, MS 38801
(601) 842-7669

Trace State Park
Route 1, Box 254
Belden, MS 38826
(601) 489-2958

Wall Doxey State Park
Route 5, Box 245
Holly Springs, MS 38635
(601) 252-4231

Winterville Historic Site
2415 Highway 1 North
Greenville, MS 38703
(601) 334-4684

Tourism Bureaus

Mississippi Division of
Tourism Development
PO Box 849
Jackson, MS 39205
(601) 359-3297 (main number)
(601) 359-5757 (fax)
(800) SEE-MISS (733-6477)
(information request line)
www.visitmississippi.org
tinquiry@mississippi.org

Aberdeen Visitors Bureau
PO Box 288
Aberdeen, MS 39730
(662) 369-9440
(800) 634-3538
www.aberdeenms.org
info@aberdeenms.org

Booneville Area Chamber/
  Tourism
PO Box 927
Booneville, MS 38829
(662) 728-4130
(800) 300-9302
www.boonevillemississippi.com
chamber@booneville
mississippi.com

Brookhaven/Lincoln County
  Chamber of Commerce
PO Box 978
Brookhaven, MS 39602-0978
(601) 833-1411
(800) 613-4667
www.brookhavenms.com
brookcham@tislink.com

Canton Convention and
  Visitors Bureau
PO Box 53
Canton, MS 39046
(601) 859-1307
(800) 844-3369

www.cantontourism.com
canton@cantontourism.com

Cleveland-Bolivar County
  Chamber of Commerce/
  Tourism
PO Box 490
Cleveland, MS 38732-0490
(662) 843-2712
(800) 295-7473
www.visitclevelandms.com
chline@cableone.net

Clinton Chamber of Commerce
PO Box 143
Clinton, MS 39060
(601) 924-5912
(800) 611-9980
www.clintonchamber.org
info@clintonchamber.org

Coahoma County Tourism
  Commission
1540 Desoto Avenue
PO Box 160
Clarksdale, MS 39614-0160
(662) 627-7337
(800) 626-3764
www.clarksdale.com
ccoc@gmi.net

Columbus-Lowndes
  Convention and Visitor's
  Bureau
PO Box 789
Columbus, MS 39703
(601) 329-1191
(800) 327-2686
www.columbus-ms.org
ccvb@columbus-ms.org

Corinth Area Tourism
  Promotion Council
PO Box 2158

Corinth, MS 38835-2158
(662) 287-8300
(662) 286-0102 (fax)
tourism@corinth.net
www.corinth.net

DeSoto County Tourism
  Association
PO Box 147
Southaven, MS 38671
(662) 429-0505
(662) 429-0390 (fax)
www.desotocountytourism.com
info@desotocountytourism.com

Greenville/Washington
  County Convention and
  Visitors Bureau
PO Box 68
Greenville, MS 38702-0068
(662) 334-2711
(800) 467-3582
www.visitgreenville.org
info@thedelta.org

Greenwood Convention and
  Visitor's Bureau
PO Drawer 739
Greenwood, MS 38935
(662) 453-9197
(800) 748-9064
www.greenwoodms.com
suzygordon@gcvb.com

Grenada Tourism Commission
PO Box 1824
Grenada, MS 38902-1824
(662) 226-2571
1-800-373-2571
gtourism@aol.com
www.grenadamississippi.com

Hattiesburg Convention and
  Visitors Bureau
One Convention Center Plaza
Hattiesburg, MS 39401
(601) 296-7475
(866) 442-8843

www.visithattie.com
tourism@hattiesburg.org

Holly Springs Tourism Bureau
104 East Gholson Avenue
Holly Springs, MS 38635
(662) 252-2515
www.visithollysprings.org

Indianola Chamber of
  Commerce
PO Box 151
Indianola, MS 38751
(662) 887-4454
(877) 816-7581
www.indianolams.org
icoc@tecinfo.com

Jackson Convention and
  Visitor's Bureau
PO Box 1450
Jackson, MS 39215-1450
(601) 960-1891
(800) 354-7695
www.visitjackson.com
info@visitjackson.com

Jackson County Chamber of
  Commerce
PO Box 480
Pascagoula, MS 39568-0480
(228) 762-3391
www.jcchamber.com
chamber@jcchamber.com

Jones County Chamber of
  Commerce
PO Box 527
Laurel, MS 39441-0527
(601) 428-0574
(800) 392-9629
www.edajones.com
edainfo@comcast.net

Kosciusko Tourist Promotion
  Council
124 N. Jackson Street
Kosciusko, MS 39090

(662) 289-2981
www.kosciuskotourism.com
kosychamber@yahoo.com

Kemper County Chamber of
 Commerce
102 Industrial Park Drive
DeKalb, MS 39328
(601) 743-2754
(601) 743-2760
www.kempercounty.com
kceda@mississippi.net

Leake County Chamber of
 Commerce
PO Box 209
Carthage, MS 39051
(601) 267-9231
(601) 267-8123
www.leakems.com
director@leakems.com

McComb Visitors Bureau
PO Box 802
McComb, MS 39649
(601) 249-0116
www.discovermccomb.com
mccombvisitorsbureau@
 mccomb-ms.gov

Meridian/Lauderdale County
 Tourism Bureau
PO Box 5313
Meridian, MS 39302
(601) 482-8001
(888) 868-7720
www.visitmeridian.com
tourism@lauderdalecounty.org

Mississippi Gulf Coast Convention and Visitor's Bureau
PO Box 6128
Gulfport, MS 39506-6128
(228) 896-6699
(800) 237-9493
www.gulfcoast.org
tourism@gulfcoast.org

Mississippi's West Coast-
 Hancock County Tourism
 Development Bureau
PO Box 3002
Bay St. Louis, MS 39521
(228) 463-9222
(800) 466-9048
www.mswestcoast.org
tourism@mswestcoast.org

Natchez Convention and
 Visitor's Bureau
640 South Canal St., Box C
Natchez, MS 39120
(601) 446-6345
(800) 647-6724
www.natchez.ms.us
ncvb@bkbank.com

Ocean Springs Chamber of
 Commerce
1000 Washington Avenue
Ocean Springs, MS 39564
(228) 875-4424
www.oceanspringschamber.com
mail@oceanspringschamber.com

Okolona Area Chamber of
 Commerce
PO Box 446
219 Main Street
Okolona, MS 38860
(662) 447-5913
www.okolona.org
patsy@okolona.org

Oxford Tourism Council
PO Box 965
Oxford, MS 38655
(662) 234-4680
(800) 758-9177
www.ci.oxford.ms.us
tourism@oxfordcenter.com

Panola Partnership, Inc.
150-A Public Square
Batesville, MS 38606
(662) 563-3126

(888) 872-6652
partnership@cableone.net

Philadelphia-Neshoba County
  Chamber of Commerce
PO Box 51
Philadelphia, MS 39350
(601) 656-1742
(601) 656-1066
www.neshoba.org
info@neshoba.org

Picayune Area Chamber of
  Commerce
PO Box 448
Picayune, MS 39466
(601) 798-3122
www.picayunechamber.org
chamber@datastar.net

Port Gibson Chamber of
  Commerce
PO Box 491
Port Gibson, MS 39150-0491
(601) 437-4351
www.portgibsonontheriver.com
portgibson_cofc@bellsouth.net

Rankin County Chamber of
  Commerce
PO Box 428
Brandon, MS 39043
(601) 825-2268
www.rankinchamber.com
gmartin@rankinchamber.com

Ridgeland Tourism Commission
PO Drawer 2358
Ridgeland, MS 39158
(601) 956-1225
(800) 468-6078
www.visitridgeland.org
info@visitridgeland.org

Starkville Visitors &
  Convention Council
322 University Drive
Starkville, MS 39759
(662) 323-3322

(800) 649-8687
www.starkville.org
request@starkville.org

Tishomingo County Tourism
  Council
1001 Battleground Drive
Iuka, MS 38852
(662) 423-0051
(800) 386-4373
www.tishomingo.org
info@tishomingo.org

Tunica County Convention
  and Visitor's Bureau
PO Box 2739
Tunica, MS 38676-2739
(662) 363-3800
(888) 488-6422
www.tunicamiss.org
tunicamiss@tunica.net

Tupelo Convention and
  Visitor's Bureau
PO Drawer 47
Tupelo, MS 38802
(662) 841-6521
(800) 533-0611
www.tupelo.net
visittupelo@tupelo.net

Vicksburg Convention and
  Visitor's Bureau
PO Box 110
Vicksburg, MS 39181-0110
(601) 636-9421
(800) 221-3536
www.visitvicksburg.com
mailcvb@vicksburgcvb.org

Yazoo County Convention
  and Visitor's Bureau
PO Box 186
Yazoo City, MS 39194
(662) 746-1815
(800) 381-0662
www.yazoo.org
yazoo@yazoo.org

Sources and Further Reading

General State Histories

Barnwell, Marion, ed. *A Place Called Mississippi: Collected Narratives*. Jackson, MS: University Press of Mississippi, 1997.

Bond, Bradley G. *Mississippi: A Documentary History*. Jackson, MS: University Press of Mississippi, 2005.

Busby, Westley F., Jr. *Mississippi: A History*. Wheeling, IL: Harlan Davidson, Inc., 2006.

Loewen, James W. and Charles Sallis, eds. *Mississippi: Conflict and Change*. New York, NY: Random House, Inc., 1974.

McLemore, Richard Aubrey, ed. *A History of Mississippi*. 2 vols. Hattiesburg, MS: University and College Press of Mississippi, 1973.

Sansing, David G. *Mississippi: Its People and Culture*. Minneapolis, MN: T. S. Denison & Co., 1981.

Skates, John Ray. *Mississippi: A Bicentennial History*. New York, NY: Norton, 1979.

Other General Histories

Crocker, Mary Wallace. *Historic Architecture in Mississippi*. Jackson, MS: University Press of Mississippi, 1973.

Polk, Noel, ed. *Mississippi's Piney Woods: A Human Perspective*. Jackson, MS: University Press of Mississippi, 1986.

Rhodes, Lelia G. *Jackson State University: The First Hundred Years, 1877–1977*. Jackson, MS: University Press of Mississippi, 1979.

Sansing, David G. *The University of Mississippi: A Sesquicentennial History*. Jackson, MS: University Press of Mississippi, 1999.

Sansing, David G. and Carroll Waller. *A History of the Mississippi Governor's Mansion*. Jackson, MS: University Press of Mississippi, 1977.

Smith, Frank. *The Yazoo River*. New York, NY: Rinehart, 1954.

Sparks, Randy J. *Religion in Mississippi*. Jackson, MS: University Press of Mississippi, 2001.

Swain, Martha H., et al. *Mississippi Women: Their Histories, Their Lives*. Athens, GA: University of Georgia Press, 2003.

Trigg, Brenda. *125 Years at Mississippi State University: A Pictorial History of the People's University*. Jackson, MS: University Press of Mississippi, 2004.

Native Americans

Atkinson, James. *Splendid Land, Splendid People: The Chickasaw Indians to Removal*. Tuscaloosa, AL: University of Alabama Press, 2003.

Carson, James Tyler. *Searching for the Bright Path: The Mississippi Choctaws from Prehistory to Removal*. Lincoln, NE: University of Nebraska Press, 1999.

Cushman, H. B. and Angie Debo, ed. *History of the Choctaw, Chickasaw and Natchez Indians*. Reprint. Lorman, OK: University of Oklahoma Press, 1999.

Debo, Angie. *The Rise and Fall of the Choctaw Republic*. Lorman, OK: University of Oklahoma Press, 1972.

DeRosier, Arthur H., Jr. *The Removal of the Choctaw Indians*. Knoxville, TN: The University of Tennessee Press, 1970.

Gallaway, Patricia. *Choctaw Genesis: 1500–1700.* Lincoln, NE: University of Nebraska Press, 1998.

Gibson, Arrell Morgan. *Chickasaws.* Lorman, OK: University of Oklahoma Press, 1971.

Hudson, Charles G. *The Southeastern Indians.* Knoxville, TN: University of Tennessee Press, 1976.

Reeves, Carolyn, ed. *The Choctaw Before Removal.* Jackson, MS: University Press of Mississippi, 2004.

Wells, Mary Ann. *Native Land: Mississippi, 1540–1798.* Jackson, MS: University Press of Mississippi, 1994.

Early Explorers and Settlers

Clayton, Lawrence A., Vernon James Knight, Fr., and Edward C. Moore, eds. *The De Soto Chronicles: The Expedition of Hernando de Soto to North America in 1539–1543.* 2 vols. Tuscaloosa, AL: University of Alabama Press, 1993.

Coates, Robert M. *The Outlaw Years: The History of the Land Pirates of the Natchez Trace.* Reprint. Whitefish, MT: Kessinger Publishing, 2004.

Crouse, Nellis M. *LeMoyne d'Iberville: Soldier of New France.* Ithaca, NY: Cornell University Press, 1954.

Daniels, Jonathan. *Devil's Backbone: Story of the Natchez Trace.* Reprint. Gretna, LA: Pelican Press, 1984.

Davis, William P. *A Way Through the Wilderness: The Natchez Trace and the Civilization of the Southern Frontier.* New York, NY: Harper Collins, 1995.

Galloway, Patricia Kay, ed. *LaSalle and His Legacy.* Jackson, MS: University Press of Mississippi, 2006.

Giraud, Marcel. *A History of French Louisiana: The Company of the Indies, 1723–1731.* Baton Rouge, LA: Louisiana State University Press, 1991.

Giraud, Marcel. *A History of French Louisiana: Years of Transition, 1715–1717.* Baton Rouge, LA: Louisiana State University Press, 1993.

Pritchard, James. *In Search of Empire: The French in the Americas, 1670–1730.* Cambridge, UK: Cambridge University Press, 2004.

Unser, Daniel H., Jr. *Indians, Settlers, and Slaves in a Frontier Exchange Economy: The Lower Mississippi Valley Before 1783.* Chapel Hill, NC: University of North Carolina Press, 1992.

Antebellum Era

Barney, William L. *The Secessionist Impulse: Alabama and Mississippi in 1860.* Princeton, NJ: Princeton University Press, 1974.

Clark, Thomas D. and John D. W. Guice. *The Old Southwest, 1795–1830: Frontiers in Conflict.* Norman, OK: University of Oklahoma Press, 1996.

Clayton, James D. *Antebellum Natchez.* Baton Rouge, LA: Louisiana State University Press, 1968.

Cooper, William J., Jr. *Liberty and Slavery: Southern Politics to 1860.* New York, NY: Alfred A. Knopf, 1983.

Dubay, Robert W. *John Jones Pettus.* Jackson, MS: University Press of Mississippi, 1975.

Hettle, Wallace. *Peculiar Democracy: Southern Democrats in Peace and Civil War*. Athens, GA: University of Georgia Press, 2001.

Jennings, Thelma. *The Nashville Convention: Southern Movement for Unity, 1848–1851*. Memphis, TN: Memphis State University Press, 1980.

Libby, David J. *Slavery and Frontier Mississippi, 1720–1830*. Jackson, MS: University Press of Mississippi, 2004.

May, Robert E. *John A. Quitman: Old South Crusader*. Baton Rouge, LA: Louisiana State University Press, 1985.

Miles, Edwin Arthur. *Jacksonian Democracy in Mississippi*. Chapel Hill, NC: The University of North Carolina Press, 1960.

Morris, Christopher. *Becoming Southern: The Evolution of a Way of Life, Warren County and Vicksburg, Mississippi, 1770–1860*. New York, NY: Oxford University Press, 1995.

Olsen, Christopher J. *Political Culture of Secession Mississippi: Masculinity, Honor, and the Antiparty Tradition, 1830–1860*. New York, NY: Oxford University Press, 2000.

Owens, Harry P. *Steamboats and the Cotton Economy: River Trade in the Yazoo-Mississippi Delta*. Jackson, MS: University Press of Mississippi, 2003.

Pereyra, Lillian A. *James Lusk Alcorn: Persistent Whig*. Baton Rouge, LA: Louisiana State University Press, 1966.

Polk, Noel, ed. *Natchez Before 1830*. Jackson, MS: University Press of Mississippi, 1989.

Ranck, James Byrne. *Albert Gallatin Brown: Radical Southern Nationalist*. Philadelphia, PA: Porcupine Press, 1974.

Walther, Eric H. *The Fire Eaters*. Baton Rouge, LA: Louisiana State University Press, 1992.

The Civil War and Reconstruction

Ballard, Michael B. *Civil War Mississippi: A Guide*. Jackson, MS: University Press of Mississippi, 2000.

———. *Vicksburg: The Campaign That Opened the Mississippi*. Chapel Hill, NC: University of North Carolina Press, 2003

Bearss, Edwin C. *Decision in Mississippi: Mississippi's Important Role in the War Between the States*. Jackson, MS: Mississippi Commission on the War Between the States, 1962.

———. *The Campaign for Vicksburg*. 3 vols. Dayton, OH: Morningside House, Inc., 1986.

Bearss, Margie Riddle. *Sherman's Forgotten Campaign: The Meridian Expedition*. Baltimore, MD: Gateway Press, Inc., 1987.

Bynum, Victoria E., *The Free State of Jones: Mississippi's Longest Civil War*. Chapel Hill, NC: University of North Carolina Press, 2001.

Carter, Samuel, III. *The Final Fortress: The Campaign for Vicksburg, 1862–1863*. New York, NY: St. Martin's Press, 1980.

Cozzens, Peter. *The Darkest Days of the War: The Battles of Iuka and Corinth*. Chapel Hill, NC: University of North Carolina Press, 1997.

Daniel, Larry J. *Shiloh: The Battle That Changed the Civil War*. New York, NY: Simon and Schuster, 1997.

Davis, William C. *Jefferson Davis: The Man and His Hour*. New York, NY: HarperCollins, 1991.

Dossman, Steven Nathaniel. *Campaign for Corinth: Blood in Mississippi.* Abilene, TX: McWhiney Foundation Press, 2006.

Engle, Stephen D. *Struggle for the Heartland: The Campaigns from Fort Henry to Corinth.* Lincoln, NE: University of Nebraska Press, 2001.

Foner, Eric. *A Short History of Reconstruction.* New York, NY: Harper Collins, 1990.

Frankel, Noralee. *Freedom's Women: Black Women and Families in Civil War Era Mississippi.* Bloomington, IN: Indiana University Press, 1999.

Harris, William C. *Day of the Carpetbagger: Republican Reconstruction in Mississippi.* Baton Rouge, LA: Louisiana State University Press, 1979.

Hurst, Jack. *Nathan Bedford Forrest: A Biography.* New York, NY: Alfred A Knopf, 1993.

Lemann, Nicholas. *Redemption: The Last Battle of the Civil War.* New York, NY: Farrar, Straus and Giroux, 2006.

Sword, Wiley. *Shiloh: Bloody April.* New York, NY: William Morrow and Co., Inc., 1974.

Wayne, Michael. *The Reshaping of Plantation Society: The Natchez District, 1860–1880.* Baton Rouge, LA: Louisiana State University Press, 1983.

Wheeler, Richard. *The Siege of Vicksburg.* New York, NY: Thomas Y. Crowell Co., 1978.

Wynne, Ben. *A Hard Trip: A History of the 15th Mississippi Infantry, CSA.* Macon, GA: Mercer University Press, 2003.

———. *Mississippi's Civil War: A Narrative History.* Macon, GA: Mercer University Press, 2003.

Into the Modern Era

Barry, John M. *Rising Tide: The Great Mississippi Flood of 1927 and How It Changed America.* New York, NY: Simon and Schuster, 1998.

Cobb, James C. *The Most Southern Place on Earth: The Mississippi Delta and the Roots of Regional Identity.* New York, NY: Oxford University Press, 1992.

Cresswell, Stephen. *Rednecks, Redeemers, and Race: Mississippi After Reconstruction, 1877–1917.* Jackson, MS: University Press of Mississippi, 2006.

Fickle, James E. *A Photographic History of Mississippi Forestry.* Jackson, MS: University Press of Mississippi, 2004.

Harrison, Alferdteen B. *Piney Woods School: An Oral History.* Jackson, MS: University Press of Mississippi, 2005.

Holmes, William F. *The White Chief: James Kimble Vardaman.* Baton Rouge: Louisiana State University Press, 1970.

Hughes, Dudley J. *Oil in the Deep South: A History of the Oil Business in Mississippi, Alabama, and Florida, 1859–1945.* Jackson, MS: University Press of Mississippi, 1993.

Kirwan, Albert. *Revolt of the Rednecks: Mississippi Politics, 1876–1925.* New York, NY: Harpers Torchbooks, 1951.

Lublin, David. *The Republican South: Democratization and Partisan Change.* Princeton, NJ: Princeton University Press, 2004.

Minor, Bill. *Eyes on Mississippi: A Fifty Year Chronicle of Change.* Jackson,

MS: J. Prichard Morris Books, 2001.

Mitchell, Dennis J. *Mississippi Liberal: A Biography of Frank E. Smith*. Jackson, MS: University Press of Mississippi, 2001.

Morgan, Chester. *Redneck Liberal: Theodore Bilbo and the New Deal*. Baton Rouge, LA: Louisiana State University Press, 1985.

Ownby, Ted. *American Dreams in Mississippi: Consumers, Poverty, & Culture, 1830–1998*. Chapel Hill, NC: University of North Carolina Press, 1999.

———. *Subduing Satan: Religion, Recreation, and Manhood in the Rural South, 1865–1920*. Chapel Hill, NC: University of North Carolina Press, 1993.

Willis, John C. *Forgotten Time: The Yazoo-Mississippi Delta After the Civil War*. Charlottsville, VA: University of Virginia Press, 2000.

Wilson, Charles Reagan. *Baptized in Blood: The Religion of the Lost Cause, 1865–1920*. Athens, GA: The University Press of Georgia, 1980.

Civil Rights

Bolton, Charles C. *The Hardest Deal of All: The Battle over School Integration in Mississippi, 1870–1980*. Jackson, MS: University Press of Mississippi, 2005.

Burner, Eric R. *And Gently He Shall Lead Them: Robert Parris Moses and Civil Rights in Mississippi*. New York, NY: New York University Press, 1995.

Cagin, Seth and Philip Dray. *We Are Not Afraid: The Story of Goodman, Schwerner, and Chaney, and the Civil Rights Campaign for Mississippi*. New York, NY: Nation Books, 2006.

Doyle, William. *An American Insurrection: The Battle of Oxford, Mississippi, 1962*. New York, NY: Doubleday, 2001.

Hendrickson, Paul. *Sons of Mississippi: A Story of Race and Its Legacy*. New York, NY: Alfred A. Knopf, 2003.

Huie, William Bradford. *Three Lives in Mississippi*. Jackson, MS: University Press of Mississippi, 2000.

Katagiri, Yasuhiro. *The Mississippi State Sovereignty Commission: Civil Rights and States' Rights*. Jackson, MS: University Press of Mississippi, 2001.

Mars, Florence. *Witness in Philadelphia*. Baton Rouge, LA: Louisiana State University Press, 1989.

Marsh, Charles. *God's Long Summer: Stories of Faith and Civil Rights*. Princeton, NJ: Princeton University Press, 1997.

McCord, William Maxwell. *Mississippi: The Long Hot Summer*. New York, NY: Norton, 1965.

Moody, Anne, *Coming of Age in Mississippi*. New York, NY: Dial Press, 1968.

Nossiter, Adam. *Of Long Memory: Mississippi and the Murder of Medgar Evers*. New York, NY: De Capo Press, 2002.

Sugarman, Tracy. *Strangers at the Gates: A Summer in Mississippi*. New York, NY: Hill and Wang, 1966.

Taylor, William Banks. *Down on Parchman Farm: The Great Prison in the Mississippi Delta*. Columbus, OH: Ohio State University Press, 1999.

Webb, Clive. *Fight Against Fear: Southern Jews and Black Civil Rights*. Athens, GA: University of Georgia Press, 2001.

Wirt, Frederick M. *We Ain't What We Was: Civil Rights in the New South*. Durham, NC: Duke University Press, 1997.

Mississippi's Cultural Heritage

Abbott, Dorothy, ed. *Mississippi Writers: An Anthology*. Jackson, MS: University Press of Mississippi, 1991.

Baker, Lewis, *The Percys of Mississippi: Politics and Literature in the New South*. Baton Rouge, LA: Louisiana State University Press, 1983.

Black, Patti Carr. *Art in Mississippi, 1790–1980*. Jackson, MS: University Press of Mississippi, 1998.

Black, Patti Carr and Marion Barnwell. *Touring Literary Mississippi*. Jackson, MS: University Press of Mississippi, 2002.

Cheseborough, Steve. *Blues Traveling: The Holy Sites of Delta Blues*, 2nd edition. Jackson, MS: University Press of Mississippi, 2004.

Cohn, Lawrence. *Nothing But the Blues: the Music and the Musicians*. New York, NY: Abbeville, 1993.

Fabre, Michel. *Richard Wright: Books and Writers*. Jackson, MS: University Press of Mississippi, 1990.

Guralnick, Peter. *Last Train to Memphis: The Rise of Elvis Presley*. London, UK: Abacus, 1995.

King, Larry L. *In Search of Willie Morris: The Mercurial Life of a Legendary Writer and Editor*. New York, NY: Public Affairs, 2006.

Lomax, Alan. *The Land Where the Blues Began*. Reprint. New York, NY: Pantheon Books, 1993.

Marrs, Suzanne. *Eudora Welty: A Biography*. Orlando, FL: Harcourt, 2005.

Palmer, Robert. *Deep Blues*. Reprint. New York, NY: Penguin, 1981.

Parini, Jay. *One Matchless Time: A Life of William Faulkner*. New York, NY: Harper Perennial, 2005.

Pinson, Patricia, ed. *The Art of Walter Anderson*. Jackson, MS: University Press of Mississippi, 2003.

Porterfield, Nolan. *Jimmie Rodgers: The Life and Times of America's Blue Yodeler*. Champaign, IL: University of Illinois Press, 1992.

Wald, Elijah. *Escaping the Delta: Robert Johnson and the Invention of the Blues*. New York, NY: Amistad, 2004.

Welty, Eudora. *On William Faulkner*. Jackson, MS: University Press of Mississippi, 2003.

Index of Place Names